COZY

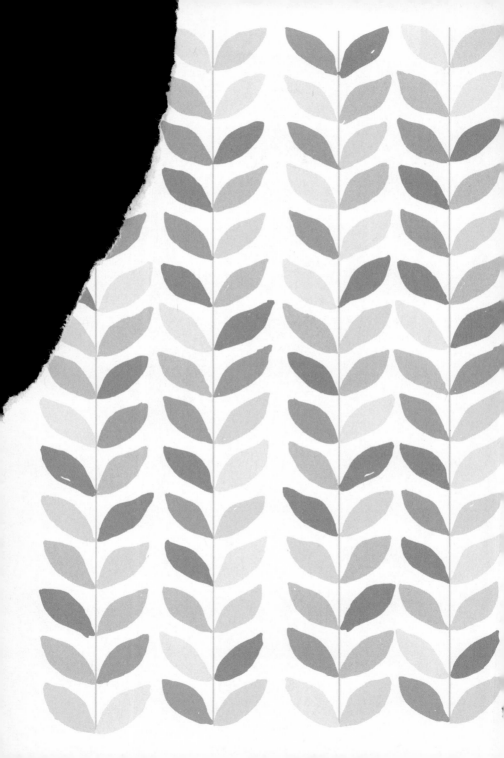

COZY

*The Art of Arranging
Yourself in the World*

ISABEL GILLIES

HARPER WAVE
An Imprint of HarperCollinsPublishers

HarperCollins books may be purchased for educational, business, or sales promotional use. For information, please email the Special Markets Department at SPsales@harpercollins.com.

Metropolitan Museum of Art Banana Bread recipe excerpt from *A Culinary Collection from The Metropolitan Mjuseum of Art* published by The Metropolitan Museum of Art, New York © 1973. Reprinted by permission.

FIRST EDITION

Designed by Fritz Metsch

Illustrations by Isabel Gillies

Library of Congress Cataloging-in-Publication Data has been applied for.

ISBN 978-0-06-265415-1

19 20 21 22 23   LSC   10 9 8 7 6 5 4 3 2 1

For my parents, Linda and Arch Gillies

CONTENTS

CONTENTS

THE RECIPES

COZY

INTRODUCTION

❧

A BOOK CALLED COZY. Really? On a planet where people are hungry and elephants endangered, perhaps other books are needed. But this is the book I thought to write because being cozy makes me feel capable of getting through to the next moment, to help another, to accomplish something important—even to love. It's easy to dismiss cozy as a confluence of hot chocolate, a roaring fire, and falling snow—magical, tangible treats you can find in a ski lodge in Vermont. *Or*, you might think coziness happens if you're lucky. Say you inherit your father's fisherman's sweater, or the stars align and you get to hold hands with a wonderful person. But I don't think it's only physical things or fortunate circumstances. I think cozy is a deeper beat, derived from a parent, a friend, a teacher, or your own good instincts.

Our three children, Hugh, Sage, and Thomas, are growing up faster than I thought. Life with them is getting away from me like a darting firefly.

On a chilly autumn day a couple of years ago, I was standing at the stove thinking about the kids. They would soon roll in, one after another. You know teenagers—they're awesome, but they have their stuff. They grapple with life, and like rock climbers on a multipitch cliff, they search for the next place to grab hold of and hoist. Sometimes I can help them, sometimes I can't, but I thought that at the very least, it would be cozy for them to be met with something simmering on a burner when they flung open the door. Whatever mama blunder I would inevitably make later that evening, or homework tangle they would be working through, the soup vibe in the apartment would be a cozy baseline supporting *all of it*, even if it didn't register with them.

Standing over the pot pulverizing the burnt-orange chunks into stock (if you don't know how to make stock, I will tell you at the end of this book—I make stock almost as much as I brush my hair), I imagined what was to come. In a blink, these kids would no longer be living with us, and however imperfect I am as a mother, I think I'm pretty good at making them cozy. Soon it would be up to them. Biting on the end of the wooden spoon, I worried: Did they know how? Sometimes I would find them reading with the overhead light blaring and shade pulled down. Their beds were often left unmade. I didn't think any of them could make a proper cup of tea. Had I taught them? Did they understand that coziness doesn't just appear out of thin air? That it's a constant endeavor, it changes in the light, it readjusts as you grow, and when you get to know yourself it takes on new meanings?

Cozy is such an inherent part of my life it feels like something everyone on the planet has a relationship with—but do they? And what is it really? I can rattle off a list of what *I* identify as cozy: cooking almost anything, community gardens, study hall, jury duty, paper coffee cups, the bus, chance meetings, reading glasses, practicing, Korean frozen pancakes, rivers, acoustic guides, lunch with girlfriends, reading aloud to a kid, taking a bath, handwriting, mailboxes, public school, TV, a made bed, writing on a train, birds, cobblestones, marriage, copyediting, the click of a radio dial, fog, toasted bran muffins, singing, the royal family, going to the movies, ferries, X-ray robes, uniforms, cookbooks. All of it is absolutely soothing to me, and as easy to overlook as pencils on a desk. It's probably best not to overlook pencils, though.

Why *are* pencils cozy? And does everyone think fog is cozy? Perhaps not. Then what *do* they think is cozy? Where does it all come from? What I started to think about on that November afternoon—and what I'm now convinced of—is how coziness stems from the very core of our individuality. Cozy is an attitude, not a thing—a shortcut to bringing the most essential parts of ourselves with us wherever we go. Once you put your finger on what makes you feel solid, supported, and calm, you can arrange yourself in a world that can be cold, awkward, dangerous, inauthentic, and unpredictable. And it doesn't have to be dramatic—there is an infinite need for coziness in any ordinary old day. Either way, coziness is something you can name and put to use, even at life's darkest hours. Perhaps it's in those hours that we most need to call on our authentic selves.

Digging a little deeper into the word, I unearthed themes: connection, control, temperature, and organization. During the writing of this book, I thought about these themes every day, and how I could use them. They were very useful in more dire times when cozy was elusive, like in Denmark, or when my father was ill.

We might not always have enough natural warmth, fortitude, or strength to traverse every bump on the road. But if we know how to create cozy using what's inside us, we can search for it on the outside no matter where we are, and each day stack the odds in our favor for happiness and, on some days, survival.

* * *

A COUPLE OF years ago, I signed up to chaperone a trip with Hugh's ninth-grade Global Studies class. The humanitarian organization Doctors Without Borders set up an interactive exhibition in Lower Manhattan to shine a light on the global refugee crisis and the more than sixty-eight million displaced peoples across the globe. For people like me who needed a wake-up call, they did a spectacular job using video, photographs, digital technology, and real materials brought from refugee camps and rescue missions. They also told true stories of refugees that I will remember forever.

Our leader was Dr. Stewart, an ob-gyn who had worked mostly in Sudan, South Sudan, and Nigeria. Her first name was Africa. We were all assigned a specific displaced person's identity. Africa showed us a wall covered with laminated pictures of personal belongings, and asked us to choose five items we would take along. When people are forced to leave their homes, they often have only minutes to prepare for an unknowable journey. They must decide quickly what they will want or need. Medicine? A mobile phone? A photograph? She told us that many people, although they know deep down they may never see their home again, bring the keys to their front door. We had five minutes to pick a few laminated pictures off the wall. I chose sneakers and my passport.

I am not qualified to write about the refugee crisis, nor will I try. But coziness comes into play here, and this exhibit demonstrated how it's necessary and at the very core of who we are—worldwide. At the end of the experience, bruised and stunned by the exhibition of cholera beds and rubber rafts, we visited a reconstruction of a tent from a refugee camp. I bent down and peered around the flap at the opening. The very first place my eyes fell was a neatly made bed. Next to it was another, smaller tidy bed. There was a rag doll lying with its carefully crafted head resting on the lumpy sack of a pillow. I looked at Africa, and she said, smiling to the group, "Moms and Dads make toys for their children out of whatever they can find—it's amazing, really, what you see." The teenagers crossed their arms around their notebooks, looking shamefully at the pitiful conditions. Some took pictures with their phones, and a few of the girls leaned on one another, reminding me of scenes in newspapers when something downright awful has happened in a high school. What I saw in the tent was evidence of the four themes of cozy.

"Excuse me," I said to Africa, "I'm sorry, but—well, I'm the class-trip mom?"

"Yes," she said patiently.

"Well, please don't take this the wrong way . . ." Her eyebrows lifted in the way people do when you apologize before you've even spoken.

"I *certainly* don't want to say the refugee crisis is cozy"— even breathing the words felt so incredibly stupid I must have been the color of borscht, "but"——more perfectly under-standable eyebrow lifting——"I couldn't help but notice, well, how *neatly* and *cozily* the beds were made in the tents, and I was just wondering if people, when they arrive, well——is there an attempt on their part, even in these circumstances, to be, um"——I could barely get the word out——"cozy?" I pre-pared for a mighty wallop.

"*YES!*" Her response reminded me of my teacher's reaction when I would get an answer correct in algebra class——it was such a rare occurrence, she was sometimes inappropriately enthusiastic. "Yes! That's what we see ev-ery day: people *absolutely* try to make themselves cozy, because that's normal, it's a basic human need——and some-thing we want people to know. These people are just like you and me. One of the first things they do is make their living spaces cozy for themselves and their family. They make the beds, just like we would; they organize their few possessions; they have proper meals with their families, even though there isn't enough food. They're people like us, it's just that they're being forced from their homes. In most cases they do what we or anyone we know would do, they try to make it all right."

If I was experiencing any insecurity about writing a book called *Cozy*, especially in light of the work that Dr. Stewart is doing, her validation gave me the fortitude to carry on.

RIDING THE BROADWAY local subway line in my hometown of New York City is the epitome of cozy. The reliability of one rumbling, screeching train car after another careening into the decrepit (okay, okay, they're not all decrepit) station has got to be a similar comfort that a metronome gives a musician. The mix of races, creeds, ages, socioeconomic levels, sexes all trundling along is soothing to me, like a great herd that I get to join at my stop. It's humanity, and most of the time, especially if I am worried or troubled, being close physically and mentally to humankind is what it takes to get me through. How can we persevere alone?

Once on the train, I immediately look for a corner seat—if I see one I feel lucky and, once settled, anchored. Tucked in next to the armrest, I pull out the article stuck into my bag before I left. If it's one of those long *New Yorker* stories about pythons or weather patterns, I could happily ride all the way from the Upper West Side to Brooklyn. I'll tell you why those nine-thousand-word articles are cozy—besides being detailed and informative, the person who wrote it, and everyone else working at the magazine, put energy, research, and smarts into it. On a cellular level, I perceive that mojo and something deep inside me is rubbed. It reminds me of falling asleep in the car as a kid—my mother or father always threw a parka or blanket over me, and even though I was dreaming, I could sense someone taking care of me. Those articles check the same box because the writers, by providing information, are looking out for you. On the subway itself, the rhythm of the stations passing, the abrupt opening of doors, the eavesdropping on neighboring conversations, the orange seats and black floor, the announcements about public safety and courtesy, is a biosphere of coziness. That train is a go-to if I'm feeling upset, unhinged, or undone. You might

be saying, *BS, if you're upset, you don't go find a subway and hop on*, to which I'm saying, *Yes, actually I do*. And the big reason why: identity.

My family is a bunch of straphangers! How you got where you were going on the MTA in the big city was a constant conversation in our household. Every night after school and office work were done, sitting around over drinks and cashew nuts, different tales of commuting emerged, small victories of a smooth transfer or discouraging malfunctions in an otherwise awe-inspiring system. I found love, security, and togetherness in discussions about the MTA.

The art of coziness can be learned and achieved. And that is what gives me peace when thinking about my kids going out in the world. I can breathe easy knowing that, should they choose, they can learn what it is about them that makes them comfortable, soothed, and stronger in even the most challenging times. For now, I'm in the business of pointing it out, like in the park—"Smell that pine! Isn't it great that even in New York City we can be close to nature?" Or, "If you pull the shade up, you can see the afternoon light." Or, "I see how you like folding the warm clothes from the dryer—isn't it satisfying how the wrinkles come out?" Soon it will be up to them.

✴ ✴ ✴

THIS BOOK GERMINATED a long time ago, when I went through a divorce. In important ways, coziness got me through that curdling time. All is fine now, but then, my life with very small children and a husband was crumbling. During one of the last meals we had together, I ate an outlandish stack of pancakes. When the never-have-seen-something-like-it-since pancakes arrived with asparagus, Gruyere cheese, and an egg on top, I followed the waiter's strong suggestion to pour maple syrup over it *all*, even the egg. In the very first bite, something about the yolk-soaked cake, woody vegetables, and French cheese *sang* in my mouth—I let out a small shriek of joy, jolting the little ones. It was only a moment, but in that moment, I knew with certainty that if I could feel something other than hurt and fear, because of a *bite of food*, I was going to be all right. I was alive inside. I might even go as far as to say that the reason I am now gainfully employed, happily married, and have a solid life is because I was able to recognize that I could feel okay for a moment because of pancakes. It was like a puzzle piece clicking in. I could build on that moment until I was on my feet. I would have to rely on small, cozy parts of the world that, up until then, I had taken for granted to get by. Things like running my fingers along a row of spice jars, eating Chinese shrimp and snow peas take-out sitting on the kitchen counter, holding a leaf in my hand as I walked to work, or even just turning on the radio—the act of turning the dial was enough.

Being cozy isn't about being comfortable. I'm *un*comfortable at this very moment because I have a bulging C5-C6 vertebra that's ramming into some nerve around my spinal cord, causing something in there to burn like it's over a low flame. I'm anxious about one of my kids at school because the assignment he worked on all weekend is still resting on the printer. There is roiling political unrest in the country on every side—goodwill seems to be lost. I had a Mr. and Mrs. (my parents' euphemism for "argument") with my beloved husband before he left for work. To top it off, I kid you not, a car alarm is screaming its head off eight floors down on the New York City streets. *But* I am working, I have sweatpants on, I'm drinking tea, I notice the wintry clouds out my window, my bed is made, and I'll go for a walk in around an hour. With these things, I am able to withstand the uncertainty and discomfort.

In order to cope with the hard stuff, it helps to know yourself, so we're going to start by looking inward. Part I will talk about how to get in touch with your inner cozy. From there we'll ripple outward, looking at opportunities to bring your authentic self into your home, your neighborhood, and anywhere you go in the world. I'd be remiss not to talk about the difficult parts of life, as those happen frequently, so I'll do that too. And, because cozy always seems to come back to the kitchen, food and drink will fill up the rest of this book. It's not that I'm a chef or food writer, but I feel I can't create a book like this without recipes, especially that link to something personal, like my friend Mo's mother's recipe for Rainy-Day Khichuri. The truth of who I am is that I have a mother who cooks a lot, and always has. The hand that swirled wooden spoons around in sauces, chopped onions, and fed us wrote the story of coziness and food for me. Our mother/daughter relationship was a complex one at times, but never around our love of cooking, reading recipes, Julia Child, scrambled eggs, and cherries in a colander. So the end of this book is a cookbook—for my mother, and because of my mother.

I can't know what everyone will think is cozy, but, in my late forties, if I've learned anything, it's that we are all pretty much the same. Sure, I might find holding a leaf as I walk cozy because my family used to walk along the Shepaug River and my parents nudged me to notice the variety and shapes of the leaves, but someone else might find healing weight and comfort in walking with a round stone in their hand because they grew up by the shore. Maybe someone else holds on to a walking stick. We're all different, but I'm pretty sure we all want to hold on to something.

PART I
————
YOU

YOU ARE COZY

IDENTITY. THE TRUTH of who you are. Knowing yourself is at the epicenter of coziness. What makes you tick? What is your jam? Point of view? What roads have you traveled? How do you learn? Who do you love? Funnily enough, some people find coziness in things that once made them sad. I asked someone I met at a dinner party what she found cozy. While twirling spaghetti, she confided that she had a lonely childhood, and was often left by herself in a nursery. She recalled there had been a grate over a heater in the room where she sat and read. She pantomimed how she hooked her little fingers into the shining brass cover. The habit of holding on to the warmed metal was a self-soothing habit, she suspected, but now that she's a happily married mother of two with loads of friends, any time she has the opportunity, she'll hold her hand up to the grate of a heater. I suspect the warmth plays a part here, but perhaps there is a reckoning with her past as well.

The light that came into your window as a child—be it warm, cool, bright, hardly there, or blazing—could shape elements of what you can tap into later in life. But in order for that to happen, you must first *notice* the light. Coziness is in the particular. It's a good start to know that you like color, for example. But what kind of color and where? Do you like wearing a certain shade of green? Do you like to have green notebooks to write in? Would you pick a green blanket over a red one? Do you use a green pen? Would you paint a room green? Recognizing yourself is a lifetime project, and it's hard! Perhaps daunting. Here I'm telling you that in order to feel cozy you need to *know* what you're all about, but what if you don't yet know? What if you have no clue what animals you connect with, or what magazine you must have on your bedside table to make you feel all is right? I get that not knowing yourself can feel impossible, but it's something that you can discover, zone in on, and develop. There are some who are aware of what makes them tick. They're born with a strong sense of self. For these people, perhaps finding coziness comes naturally or more quickly—they have a clear pathway to their essence. Being a gal with learning disabilities, I know a little something about things not coming naturally or quickly, so it's my firm belief that people who don't have a well-defined notion about who they are, with tools, can find it, and then hone and develop the discoveries until they are well-worn and reliable.

Know Thyself

MAGGIE FLANNIGAN WAS the best acting teacher, I might even say teacher, I ever had—I think of her every day of my life. She was tough as a drill sergeant, intense as Sam Shepard, and petite. Maggie wore brown leather pants, the likes of which I thought were reserved for rock stars like Chrissie Hynde. In a second-floor studio on Third Avenue, she listened to our scenes play out with her whole body, like how some people look like conductors when they listen to music. It's funny— you would think that one would watch scenes, but she listened. If a scene was going really well, her head would come up, but mostly I remember Maggie, head down, swaying with her eyes closed. Her ear was trained for authenticity, and if you created one false note, she stopped the scene dead in its tracks like she was training dogs, never letting bad behavior continue. Living truthfully, moment to moment, was her mantra. She was direct and unapologetic with her criticism, and in the rare case when you had done something well, she was direct about that too—it felt like winning an Oscar.

Maggie taught us how to endow an inanimate object with meaning. As an actor, you work in the make-believe, and props are just props unless you inject true, precise personal meaning into them. She taught us how to be specific, as specific as a chemist.

People often assume that the meaning has to be directly related to the circumstance, but it doesn't have to be. I once played a murderer on *Law & Order*. While I was on the stand, the DA lifted up a prop knife in a bag to prove I was the perpetrator. Seeing a random prop knife wouldn't elicit any feeling in me or anyone watching, because I'm not a murderer. I had to endow it with personal meaning. I asked myself, *What if?* What if that knife had killed my brother? That did it. I was able to emotionally live truthfully during an imaginary circumstance. Even when the cameras weren't rolling, I cried my eyes out just thinking about that knife. It's the same in life. Consider: if someone says, *I love you*, that's pretty good, but it's not as good as someone saying, *I love your Long Island accent.*

Maggie understood the importance of being familiar with the specifics, and understood that knowing yourself doesn't always come naturally. So, being a great teacher, she had an exercise for us to practice.

Here's what you do: no matter where you're going, from the time you leave your door until you get to where you're going—whether it's walking to the bank or to work or to get an ice cream—form an opinion about everything you pass. Start slow: Do you like it? Do you not? Then build to the harder question: Why? What's your judgment? Walk by a man with a blue shirt, you think, *I appreciate that color blue— it's electric, fun, and you can see it from a mile away. Alternately, I don't appreciate the man's stride or his hat with no brim. Keep going. I like cracks in the sidewalk, but not if there is a weed growing out of it because that makes me think something is being ignored . . . I don't like it AT ALL when people throw wrappers on the ground . . . I like seeing a recycling bin. I like the slope of that roof and wonder how many more are like it in this neighborhood.*

Your views should be strong, abundant, and as decisive as you can make them. It's rather exhausting because you'll see that once you get going there is *so much* to have an opinion about, it almost drives you crazy. But you get good at it, and you discover that there are parts of the world that really do lift you up. In my twenties, I found that I adored mailboxes. Every solid, hardworking, dark blue receptacle sends small ripples of serenity through me. I hope that all this e-mail never does away with them. My guess is that I always liked mailboxes, but in noting their stout blue tubbiness on those walks I learned that they were a part of my everyday surroundings that I could count on to make me feel better.

To this day I rely on them to ground me. Even the throaty squeak emitted from the hinges is a comfort—it's like they say, *It's okay, I'm always here.*

Just Choose Something

HERE'S ANOTHER THING: if you really can't figure out what you have an affinity for or feel weary or daunted by the search for what turns you on, I think you can make it up. Just choose something. Close your eyes and think, "What animal (color, author, flower, etc.) would I like to zero in on to collect, identify with, or appreciate? What would I like people to associate *me* with?" When I was thirteen, there was an older girl in my school who was bragging that her beau *just knew* to give her her most favorite flower in the world, lilies of the valley. That declaration knocked my socks off. *Gosh*, I thought, *one day I hope that I will be the kind of person who has a specific flower.* Now, as it turned out, if you are my husband and you would like to give me flowers, the ones you get at the deli are huge white Casablanca lilies. That's what I ended up loving. I find their enormity and their overpowering fragrance friendly, as if they are saying, *Hello! I'm here!* BUT, if one felt lost in the flower department, there is nothing wrong with just choosing. Yellow roses, gardenias, daisies—doesn't matter. Do they make you happy? Great! Some people have a signature cocktail, like Don Draper always drank old-fashioneds—perhaps one shouldn't drink as many as he did, but still, they were his.

My parents coincidentally each gave the other spoons when they became engaged. They built on that weird accident and have endowed spoons with meanings of family, romance, and togetherness—talismans of luck and love. Now they give spoons as presents when young people get engaged. It's a fifty-year relationship with a plain old object that has taken on spiritual proportion. They didn't wake up one morning with the epiphany that spoons were a physical manifestation of their souls. They chose to play along with serendipity, and now those spoons are a cozy reminder of love, partnership, and the promise of marriage. I always have my eye out for spoons. (*Think how many spoons there are in the world.*) And all of them are cozy to me. This is low-hanging fruit, and I shamelessly pick it all the time. If I feel lost or overwhelmed, even holding a spoon in my hand will do good.

Some people connect with a city from the moment their train rolls into the station. I knew Providence would be one of my places right away as I clambered up College Hill to visit a boyfriend there. Maybe all that young love did cast a cozy glow over the city, *but* Providence also has colonial houses nestled together along cobblestone streets. It had a great sandwich shop called Mutt & Geoff's. There are multiple colleges there, so it's pulsing with people growing and learning. I ended up going to the Rhode Island School of Design and was able to draw in gently banged-up studios for eight hours a day. Providence might have started out cozy because of personal experience with young love, but then I built on it beyond the adolescent friendship. Sometimes circumstances can make something cozy, and long after the situation changes, the coziness lives on.

It might seem that people who know how to incorporate this kind of specificity into their lives are advanced or nuanced—and maybe they get a jump on cozy, but the point is, *anyone* can have a point of view. Anyone can be particular. Anyone can have something to like.

Pencils

"Erasers make forgiveness possible."
—APPLICANT FOR THE PENCIL APPRECIATION SOCIETY

PENCILS. FAMILIAR. STURDY. dependable tools that live with most of us. The humble pencil is put to good use while making lists, doodles, solving math problems, note-taking in margins of books, drawings, adjusting recipes, grading, producing fine lines, medium lines, thick lines, marking calendars, making budgets, scoring games, or lying on a desk—just the sight of a pencil is cozy. There is something about a pencil that says, *I will help you try.*

Pencils are generally wooden, a soft, warm material to hold—or bite into. Were you a biter or did you refrain? Some pencils have the name of an organization like a school imprinted into them—a small burst of institutional pride on a modest standby. You can sharpen a pencil to your liking with a variety of instruments, some small enough for your pocket, some heavy and electric, some with a handle that you get to grab on to and twirl until the right sharpness has been achieved. There are multiple brands, and a wide range of lead hardness is out there, so one can be as particular and as personal as one likes—and people are. You might think you know someone, but have you ever asked what kind of pencils they like? You can learn oodles about someone with that simple question. My upstairs neighbor is so affronted by an eraser-less pencil, if she comes across one in her house she immediately confiscates it until she is able to correct the offense with a nub eraser (she keeps a supply in her top desk drawer). Pencils come in a rainbow of colors. You can keep a pencil behind your ear or stick it in your ponytail, something I did the entire time I was a waitress.

Although for me pencils are a part of everyday life—we must have one hundred in different lengths and sharpnesses all over the apartment—for many in this computer age, pencils connect people with their childhood and schooling.

I know of a Pencil Appreciation Society, and in the essay portion of the application to join—yes, there's an application—almost every pencil-written submission details how pencils played a role in the applicant's personal growth. For some, whizzing through complicated math with the sharpest Ticonderoga #2, never needing to erase, united them with the strong and reliable side of their brain. For others, the pencil allowed the freedom to use their imagination with abandon, confident that if something didn't come out right, the eraser was standing by at the ready—a chance for another go at creativity. For others, like architects, design simply wouldn't be possible without the pencil. One applicant wrote:

"Since my birthday was August 25th and I was a schoolgirl in the 1950s, my birthday gifts were typically a new school dress and a pencil box. The dresses I've forgotten, but the pencil boxes I can remember in great detail. The snap closure, the stiff cardboard lid, the tray inside with multiple compartments for organizing supplies including a long area for pencils and shorter areas for erasers and crayons. One pencil case was deeper and had a shallow drawer that pulled out. That must have been a deluxe model. I remember feeling proud of my pencil boxes and how they demonstrated my readiness for school."

This is the application for the Pencil Appreciation Society:

PENCIL APPRECIATION SOCIETY
APPLICATION FOR MEMBERSHIP

Name:

_____

Mailing address/telephone:

Summer _____

Winter _____

Email address:

_____

In order for the PAS to determine your eligibility for membership in the Society, we ask that you provide us with the following information (pencil required):

What is your favorite brand of pencil?

○ Blackwing

○ Dixon Ticonderoga

○ Tombow

○ Faber-Castell

○ Other: _____

What hardness do you prefer?

○ #1

○ #2

○ #3

What size do you prefer?

○ Fat

○ Standard

○ Thin

○ Short (golf scoring pencil)

What color pencil do you prefer?

○ Yellow

○ Black

○ White

○ Other: _____

Do you use colored pencils? If so, what colors do you prefer?

_____

Do you use pencils with erasers?

○ Yes

○ No

If yes, what kind of eraser do you prefer?

○ Affixed, round

○ Removable

○ Other: _____

Where do you keep pencils in your house?

_____

What kind of pencil sharpener do you use?
- ○ Electric
- ○ Battery-operated
- ○ Affixed manual
- ○ Small desk manual
- ○ If possible, please give the brand name:

_____

Where is it/are they located in your house?

_____

Do you use a mechanical pencil?
- ○ Yes
- ○ No

If yes, what brand do you use?

_____

What is your favorite pencil store?

_____

Does your library include _The Pencil_ by Henry Petroski (1993)?
- ○ Yes
- ○ No

If yes, in the hardback or paper version?

_____

What famous Concord transcendentalist's family had a pencil company?

_____

Using the reverse side of this application, please write a brief essay on each of the following subjects:

Autobiographical material as it relates to the esteemed pencil.

Pencil memories.

How do you use pencils?

*All drawings in this book were done with pencils.

HERITAGE

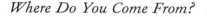

Where Do You Come From?

THE MOST OBVIOUS path to knowing yourself is looking at history, personal or generalized. This is, of course, a complicated thing to say because our histories have darkness, sorrow, mystery, and psychology woven through the loom—sometimes we don't even know what loom is ours. So, since where we came from can be so complex, let's start with beans. Knowing exactly where something comes from—like a bean—is cozy. There is a particular vendor at the farmers' market on Ninety-Seventh Street in New York who sells his heirloom beans in ziplock baggies all piled in a widemouthed wicker basket. The beans are the colors of cows: light browns, deep kidneys, cranberries, tans, and patchy black-and-whites. If you want to find matching varieties, you have to take off your mittens and sort through. As you scour for matching cranberry beans, the farmer, standing on the other side of the folding table, proudly recounts their history—it's like he's describing a child, *Check out the markings on these Scarlett Runners, they grew beautifully this year—do you know there is evidence of these guys dating back to the 1700s?* Appreciating their lineage enhances the experience of whatever you do next with them. All of a sudden, you're not just soaking random beans, you're soaking shiny pedigree beans. The ancestors of those beans could have been served to Almanzo Wilder of Laura Ingalls Wilder's *Farmer Boy* on his farm in upstate New York. (They are forever talking about beans in *Farmer Boy*.)

When we study or observe history, we see ourselves in the collective past—we can empathize. History is a way we connect to places and people we will never meet or know and, sometimes, the further you get away from yourself by looking back through generations—centuries of them even—the closer you are to knowing yourself. Think of museums: there is something comforting, even in the most violent representations, like Picasso's *Guernica*, about understanding our universally shared experiences. We may not recognize the iconography in an artifact from ancient Iraq, or in a medieval tapestry, or a Cézanne, but we can feel humanity in it. I would say that it's cozy to read the blurb beside the work of art so you can understand it better, but sometimes, as my ex-husband advised the children when they went to museums, it's beneficial just to absorb.

/ / /

HAVE YOU EVER watched the videos on 23andMe of people who had been adopted discovering their blood families? It's so moving you would have to be a robot not to weep until your shirt was damp watching sisters who have never met, cousins, half siblings comparing their hands, locating familiarity at long last. The people in the videos describe the sensation of finally knowing as finding the missing puzzle piece.

A friend who has an adopted child told me that adopted kids "snuggle up" in the story of how they came to their family. There is pain involved in the question of why you don't live every day with the person you grew inside of. It's easy to take knowing for granted—but perhaps we shouldn't because there is so much comfort in knowing. He said there is a "cosmic sense of coziness when one can rely on how connections were made, and how exactly everyone involved came together as a family." He even kept the plane ticket stub so the child can now see it, hold it, connect to it.

I was always hesitant to take one of those genetics tests. As far as I am aware, and what I've banked on for my whole life, is that my people hail from Scotland and England. Some of them came over very early in this country's beginnings, so I'll throw in Pilgrim too—I can get down with all things colonial. There was once a PBS reality series called *Colonial House* that I watched with the rapture that some watch *The Voice* or *Game of Thrones*. For me, the center of cozy is lodged in the craggy earth of the British Isles. Just thinking about scones, fish pie with green peas, moors and highlands, *Braveheart*, trucker tea, sheep, rain, fog, *Wuthering Heights*, barley, Tudor England, tartan, and trudging around in crappy weather makes me feel constitutionally sound. It's part of how I identify myself, so naturally, I bring as much Anglophilia into my life as possible. *The Great British Baking Show* is a lullaby for me. On the hardest days, it soothes me to sleep. And if there is no TV, even if I think of the theme song, I find myself cozier.

Part of the reason I like to write is because of the image

I have of Jane Austen wrapped in wool by a paned window writing about the romances of Marianne and Elinor in *Sense and Sensibility*. A dream for me is to be woken up each morning with my heart slightly shattered because someone stoic and Scottish is playing the bagpipes outside my window. (This unbelievable luxury is a daily occurrence for Her Majesty Queen Elizabeth II—don't get mad at her; she's the queen.) The ancestral ache and cultural personality has such a grip on my identity, if I took one of those genealogy tests and found out that somehow I *wasn't* genetically from the Crown dependencies it would be an unmitigated crisis. I imagine, though, after mourning the loss of my limey roots, I would pull up my argyle socks and get to the business of diving deep into the waters of wherever it is I actually came from. Knowing is far better than not knowing—always.

I did eventually take one of those genetic tests, and it turns out I have quite a lot of Scandinavian blood. I went to my father with this information with trepidation and thrill: I assumed he prided himself as being a Scotsman through and through, but knew any nuance of heritage would be of interest to him. He said without a smidge of surprise, "Haven't you ever heard of the Vikings? Invasion!"

I get that investigation can be scary—ignorance is bliss, but is it really? If we're saying that looking inward is your access to cozy, then no matter what you find it will ultimately help you, free you to welcome and cherish all parts of yourself. Go to the records!

Histories	Attics
Accents	Folklore
Tartans	Memoirs
Maps	Old letters
Family trees	Ellis Island
School records	Neighborhoods
Heirlooms—antiques	Photo albums

Peeling the Onion

HERE'S SOME MORE low-hanging cozy fruit: How were you parented? It doesn't matter if your parents were biological, adopted, uncles, grandparents, if you were raised by the state, or by the animals in the jungle like Mowgli, what happened to you growing up informs who you are more than anything else (says me, the non-shrink). This is painful to write because as a parent myself, I can't say that I have always done the best job, but even in the mistakes our parents made, or we make as parents, there is coziness to be harvested.

This might be hard to read because there are a lot of tough situations out there. And, you know what, sometimes circumstances are just un-cozy. That's okay. Only you can know what you might be able to reclaim for yourself. We may not like how we were parented or how we parent, but it behooves us to see what we can use to our advantage anyway. It would be a mistake to overlook the inherent comfort of familiarity, even if it's complex. Because I am learning disabled, the struggle that came along with those differences in my brain shaped some touchstones of what makes me feel okay now. Most of the time, really through tenth grade, I couldn't do my homework. Assignments seemed as if they were written in another language, and after a while it just got embarrassing to keep on asking for help, so I stopped. The humiliation I felt in not being able to complete tasks I knew my friends could, sent me into stratospheres of isolation—sometimes the floor was the only thing I felt I had, and I would lie on whatever one was under me, frequently. Now that I think about it, the sight of me lying on the floor probably drove my mother into her own stratospheres of frustrated sorrow. Neither of us knew what to do, so we screamed and yelled and eventually got through it, though both of us have scars. All these years later, wooden floors that have been warmed by the sun are a refuge. When faced with impossibility, I find a floor—they are always around.

Wouldn't you know it, my older son is learning disabled too. You would think that my own experiences would have made me a super parent in this department, but the opposite is true. When he struggled, I didn't understand. My empathy was overtaken by anxiety, and I had no big-picture thinking. Whatever my mother was afraid of for me, I was for him. And the impatient frustration I felt that he just couldn't *do it* got the better of me. I blamed myself for giving him the affliction, and I blamed myself for not being compassionate when you'd think I would be in the most fortunate position to do so. Where did he find comfort when I couldn't give it to him? Was it in the feeling of the woolen Berber rug in his bedroom? Was it the sound of the clothes tumbling around in the dryer in the office where he did his homework? Was it in the yo-yo he twirled and spun around his fingers when he couldn't face another page? I don't know, and maybe he won't until he is older. But I'm counting on the small things to give him comfort where I had regrettably failed.

If I peel a different layer of the onion to see how I was raised, I think about my parents embracing the unfamiliar. As a younger person, I'm not sure I contemplated the relationship between cozy and the outside world, but my mother did. On trips, even across town, like an otter teaching her baby to swim, my mother was constantly pointing out something was cozy. "Isn't it cozy that this restaurant has a hook for us to put our raincoat?" Or, while driving, "See all those cows lying down together—cows lying down means it's going to rain, you know." She would nudge me out of my elementary oblivion to make me aware of things I would later take comfort in. If we dig down to the bottom of what we consider most cozy, a lot of it comes from what happens to us in our formative years—how someone took care of you grows into how you take care of yourself. Although it's *never too late to learn coziness*. A friend of mine whose mother died when she was young said she was unmindful—unaware—of coziness until her college boyfriend's mother taught it to her, and now it's her way of life. I see her teaching her daughter how to be cozy every time we are together.

My mother, like some sort of fortune-teller, even connected us with parts of the world we had no association with, but might someday. A mezuzah is a piece of parchment inscribed with Hebrew verses from the Torah, and according to Jewish law you are supposed to have one rolled up in a small case and affixed to your door frame. We had a mezuzah attached to the doorpost of our apartment for the entire forty-five years my parents lived there. It belonged to the previous family. My mother instinctually would never take such a thing down. When we asked what it was, Mum said matter-of-factly, "Oh, it's from the family that lived here before we did—it's a Jewish prayer. I believe it protected their family and so I believe it will protect our family as well—give it a pat next time you leave. I always do."

Something Borrowed

SARIS, ROMEO AND JULIET, AND JEWS

BECAUSE I HAVE woke teenagers in the house, suddenly, as I'm writing about incorporating other people's identity into one's own life, I'm a tad concerned about rowing into the choppy waters of cultural appropriation. I don't want to. I am confused about this subject because one of the coziest things to do is try on someone else's worldview, and sometimes that worldview can become our own. The truth of who we are isn't fixed. It develops and becomes resonant as we make our way through the world. There is abundant coziness in what we learn along the way. Appreciating other people and their points of view, cultures, opinions, and particularities is cozy because it enhances who we are as a community. When we identify with others, we feel connected to them, and ourselves.

In first grade, my mother took me to an Indian seamstress

and had me fitted for a sari to wear when I delivered a report on India. I was spun, wrapped, and tucked in the jewel-colored swaths like a fly being rolled in a gossamer web by a spider. Because we lived in New York City, with its booming immigrant population, we were exposed as young children to the cultures of dozens of countries. I never thought it was bad to be steeped in someone else's identity, even if it was just for a day. Where I went to school as a young girl was close to Yorkville. If you went into some of the bakeries for dark rye bread or Black Forest cake, you could hear German being spoken. Our neighborhood on the Upper West Side was a robust mix of Jewish, Dominican, Russian, and more. No one person seemed like another. Dipping in and out of languages, customs, and clothes didn't turn anyone's head. But things have gotten tricky—there is much more opportunity to step on toes or to offend inadvertently. With that in mind, I will carefully row on because the fact of the matter is my second husband is Jewish and I'm not. Over the last decade, though, I have become Jew-*ish*.

If heritage is a linchpin of coziness, I firmly believe heritage/religion/identity can be borrowed too—it *has* to be, especially if you live in America, a country of immigrants. It's impossible not to ingest other people's way of doing things. Studying other people and their ways strengthens who you are and what you are able to hand down to others. Not to mention, if you do have a hard time pinpointing who you are, you need to keep your eyes and heart even more open.

Incorporating someone else's culture or way of life into your own isn't always easy, and it takes some effort. You are dealing with intimate traditions and comfort zones. People

have been instructed from the beginning of time to be wary
of others who do things differently. (Romeo and Juliet, anyone?) I guess it's fear of the unknown. Understandable, but,
Lord, it's easy to see how this has gotten us into irreparable
trouble. Difference comes up all the time, so how do we deal
with it? How can we make difference translate into deep connection?

When I married Peter, as in love as we were, there was a
contrast in our religions and how we were raised. There are
books written and movies made about differences, but when
you are trying to merge lives, differences can be hard. Simi-
larity and common ground is easier. When my first husband
married his new French-speaking wife, he learned French so
they could literally speak the same language. My guess is,
he partially saw it as an academic challenge, but also, it was
just cozier that way. I was recently speaking with a friend
about this subject. She said, "Something that I found so
cozy about my husband's family was the closeness to their
elders—but [it] took ages for me to acclimate. The cozy way
they respected and shower love on them—even as they are
so old. The formality of my own grandparents didn't allow
for handholding, stroking, and being cozy on an old, wrin-
kled hand and arm. I longed to be a part of it. It took a while,
but I got in there."

Nothing surprised me about marrying a Jewish man—
I'd grown up on the Upper West Side of New York City, and
thought most people were Jewish. But, even though inter-
faith marriage felt seamless in concept, Peter and I differed
culturally, and there were challenges that came along with

that setup. How do you make cultural variances cozy? You can—so much so that two Yom Kippurs ago in a quiet moment during Kol Nidre services, I asked God if I could be both Episcopalian and Jewish. He said yes (don't be furious: I always think of God as a man—I can't help it; apparently, it's Michelangelo's fault). I wasn't going to convert to Judaism as I already had two little Episcopalian boys who had been baptized, but I felt in order to make everything connected (we were a young stepfamily, after all), I wanted to open myself, be curious, and find ways to feel of like mind.

This is where *acceptance* comes into coziness.

When Peter and I were engaged, I marched right to the bookshop and invested in two or three Jewish cookbooks. One is very academic, more of an encyclopedia, a history of Jewish culture by Claudia Roden. Truthfully, I might have only cooked five recipes from it, but for the last twelve years it's something I keep close. And for the lion's share of the autumn, when a lot of Jewish holidays take place, it's on my bedside table.

I don't think Peter's ancestors would have been thrilled that his marital puzzle piece wasn't of Ashkenazi decent, but the fact was we were getting married. At first, the best way to understand the heart of his Jewishness wasn't through a rabbi (that would come later) but through brisket. Because of his mother's generosity, I quickly (maybe two years in) was given a holiday to host. This is a big deal. I got Rosh Hashanah, which is nothing to sneeze at.

The first year, I organized myself to the point of making an itinerary for the groceries: *nine a.m.: Fairway for vegeta-*

bles and apples; pick up brisket from butcher at eleven fifteen. It felt like playing house. As a child, if you were even twenty minutes into a good game of house, you felt so invested in the characters and relationships you and your friends imagined, they were as real as the nose on your face. As ten-year-olds, we would make "stews" out of snow and pine needles, and give them to our "children." If you played make-believe for long enough, families, loves, complex interpersonal relationships came to life, and of course you had to cook for them. This is what it was like in the early years when I prepared the Rosh Hashanah dinner. It would take imagination and goodwill for this shiksa to become the *balabusta* I so wanted to be. It was in the doing that I became—sort of. Not fully, of course, but hopefully more than ten years of observing my Rosh Hashanah dinners, resplendent with crisp apples, orange blossom honey, and the most layered, flavorful beef brisket my Waspy self can braise, his *mishpocha* have come around.

Since year one, for most Jewish holidays, save for Rosh Hashanah, the five of us pile in the minivan midafternoon, balancing flourless chocolate-walnut cookies, artisanal matzo bread from the bakery on 105th Street, or something sloshy like applesauce (I have a very simple recipe for applesauce that is essential to all kinds of happiness, and it's at the end of the book) and drive fearlessly into the Lincoln Tunnel alongside thousands of other families, out to Livingston, New Jersey, to Aunt Terri and Uncle Bob's. The house is not unlike the *Brady Bunch* house, and it's just as warm. Our son Hugh once said of his stepfamily, "In a Jewish household it sounds like there is music playing even if there isn't." These holidays felt NOTHING like the ones I knew, but if I was going to be cozy there, I had to absorb— not always easy because a knee-jerk reaction to difference often turns people into Teflon. Milling around the kitchen are aunts with fresh manicures and soft sweaters, uncles on their iPhones and holding babies, cousins in braces, and the new boyfriends trying to appear helpful. The discussion is traffic, college applications, sports, politics (lightly), health, and family news all at once. The real *balabustas* boss around about what needs to get warmed up, kids run up and down the plush carpeted stairs to the rec-room basement, and there is lots of lifting tinfoil and picking at the baking dishes of kugel waiting to be put on the table. "Who made this one?" a nibbler will call (or yell) across the white Formica center island. "The apricot is Aunt Sascha's!" The nibbler raises their eyebrows in approval and pilfers another taste.

As fun, familial, and close as it really is, at first my two boys and I were strangers in a strange land. Did I feel cozy? Not really. I could see how it all could be, but it felt out of reach. How could I get close? How could my children? Ironically, the time when I felt most like a square peg trying to fit into the round hole was at dessert time. Once the Shofar has been stored back in the drawers, and brisket is cleared into the kitchen, the dessert gets paraded in. Think of Noah's Ark: there are two of everything on that table. Pillowy macaroons, dense apple cakes, my mother-in-law's revered sugar cookies—some with jam, some with chocolate chips—Bundt cakes, chocolate-covered matzo, zucchini breads, babkas, rugelach, cupcakes, black-and-whites, and my sister-in-law's tire-sized fruit tray. (And at Passover there are only flourless desserts.) It looks like a school bake sale on Election Day. My people have *one* dessert, even on the biggest holidays. And by "dessert," I mean a pear that you eat with a fork and knife. As a newly engaged woman, I was bewildered by the outpouring of confections and unsettled at the lack of traditions to which I was accustomed. Black-and-white cookies, but no wine to speak of? Three different apple cakes, but not one heated political argument? Banana pudding, but served to the tune of seventeen different-yet-simultaneous conversations? How could a family dinner be cozy if you don't go around the table asking who everyone thinks should run in the next presidential election? This was uncharted territory. And as far as I could see in Peter's family, the dessert portion was the height of coziness for everyone around me. I *had* to understand. This was my family! My stepdaughter is Jewish, so I even had a Jewish kid!

In learning how to be cozy, you are responsible for taking what happens to you (i.e., marrying someone from a different culture), learning from it, then connecting it to your innermost self. When I got home, feeling like a disenfranchised oddball, sitting in my kitchen was that Claudia Roden cookbook. I had been using it to make a string bean dish I brought that night. I put the tome under my arm and went to draw a bath (more on those later—a good soak aides in healing most quandaries). I knew the author would guide me, I just didn't think I would need help understanding chocolate. After my bath, sitting with knees up next to a sleeping Jewish husband, I probed. On page 146 was a chapter about sweets—a big one.

"Jews are known for their fondness of sweet things . . . They represent joy and happiness and have to be present at festive and happy occasions."

So there it was. As much as I believe people are all the same, there are nuances, shifts, and dividing forces at work that separate us. A lot of time you need help in being cozy together. It's like studying for an exam: you won't do very well if you just sit in the classroom. It takes more work; you have to read the book—and underline.

Apple Cake
Hamantaschen
Rugelach
Babka
Chocolate Covered Matzo
Sufganiyot
Macaroons
Ellen's cookies
Gelt

raspberry or chocolate chip
jam?

Honey Jar

PART II

HOME

"It is the simple things of life that make living worthwhile, the sweet fundamental things such as love and duty, work and rest and living close to nature."

—LAURA INGALLS WILDER

I HAD AN English teacher in eleventh grade who taught us about "sense of place." A sense of place is important when you study writing because often a character's identity is strongly connected to the geography, or location. There is meaning in what surrounds them. Ms. Shutt was relating the terminology to writing, but what struck me about it, and why I've kept the term close by all these years later, was the universality of the phrase. Most people have a sense of place that orients them. Doesn't matter where or what that place is. Whatever is closest to you physically, where you dwell—that's probably your place. The rhythms of private time in the home, what you have chosen to surround yourself with and their functions, can be dependable touchstones. Doorstops, frying pans, rugs, windows, and laundry detergent are workhorses of cozy, and not to be overlooked. There is a reason you chose the pot holder you chose. Is it red and cheerful, making every time you open the drawer and see it a pleasure? Does it remind you of the pot holders you had growing up? Does it fit your hand in a satisfying way? Do you love that it's protective when you are trying to do something tricky, like stick your hand in a 400-degree oven? Somehow that potholder can reflect yourself back to you, if you let it.

In my apartment, there is one corner of an IKEA sofa that waits for me every morning to support whatever the day has brought. Right next to it is a small table with a space for a mug. Not one part about it is fancy or even particularly pretty, but it's almost like it has a sign on it that says, *IG*. Have I personalized it? I guess so—something deep in my constitution is righted every time I go there to gather thoughts, check e-mail, or pat a dog. I have a sense of place in that nook; I know who I am. I didn't plan for it, and now I seek it out every day. Does this make me stronger? Happier? Better able to deal? Maybe. I never underestimate the power of coziness—it's like the sun for Superman.

MAKING THE BED

"A friend of mine remembers being counseled by her elderly aunt long ago that even if she found herself in poverty or sickness, she should always make a good bed for herself."

—CHERYL MENDELSON (AUTHOR OF *Home Comforts, The Art and Science of Keeping House*, A BOOK I KEEP ALONG WITH MY COOKBOOKS AS IT COMES IN HANDY MORE OFTEN THAN ONE WOULD THINK)

I AM NOT TIDY by nature. It's been a mighty struggle since I was little to keep my bedroom organized and put away. I love it when things are clean, and I have a *much* easier time keeping bathrooms and kitchens clean—I look forward to whipping a fridge into shape, and I even find cleaning a toilet quite satisfying. But bedrooms are hard for me. I *loathe* putting my clothes away. So I don't say this lightheartedly, or primly, but I believe in it to my very core: coziness starts with a made bed. Thematically it makes sense because making one's bed is all about control, connection, and identity. Some people say if you want to see who someone is, look at their wallet; I say look at the bed. Maybe it's both.

The messiest my rooms ever got were from ages eighteen to twenty-six. With no parental oversight, weird hours, and the freedom of a slightly unhinged young-adult life, my clothes rose sky-high in the middle of college dorm rooms and studio apartments like something out of *Animal House*. I think it appalled some boyfriends, and it definitely grossed out my ladylike apartment mates, which makes me shudder with shame—but I was still learning. However, my bed, even if it was a futon on the ground, was *always* made. Full-sized bed, with a quilted mattress cover, white bottom sheet, white top sheet smoothed and pulled to the top, a duvet encased with a Tree of Life tapestry, sheet folded over it at the top. Two pillows with white covers and a big purple Indian-print European square centered between them. As is true with so many things, this was definitely my mother's influence. She sees bed making not as a staunch, uptight rule of law, but as an easy opportunity to provide yourself with peace of mind and a sense of self.

Back in those days, I was a bit of a rock-and-roll groupie. Bands like Blues Traveler and Spin Doctors were playing nightly all over the East and West Village, where I lived. If I said I went to see them every night, I don't think I'm exaggerating. Dancing in the wee hours, jammed into beer-soaked, sweaty, hormonal bars and then waifing around on the streets, smoking too many cigarettes and eating hummus on MacDougal Street at two a.m. was a wonderful adventurous exploration, perhaps a bit rebellious, into the wild for me, but it could also be a little unsettling. Who did I think I was, Janis Joplin? I wasn't—and I didn't want to be. But when you are forming, as one does in their twenties, sometimes it's hard to tell exactly who you are. When I returned to my apartment, sometimes reeling, and saw my cozy, "dressed" bed, I was reminded that no, I wasn't going to fall off the side of the earth into a sea of Jägermeister and (marvelous) long-haired guitar players. I was going to stay on my path, carve out my own occupations, habits, and relationships, and get a good sleep. Somehow the person I was striving to be was tucked in neatly with the quilts. The made bed gave me confidence I would find her one day.

We need look no further than the animal kingdom to see that making a bed is deeply instinctual. Primates such as gorillas and chimpanzees build nests daily. Entire families of mountain gorillas have been videoed carefully pulling leaves and branches together, layering, weaving, and building so they are supported through the uncertain night. There is decision-making and time put into these intricate and sturdy cradles. Orangutan babies observe their mothers building nests from the time they are six months old and only become proficient when they are three! According to the Jane Goodall Institute, chimps construct nests not only for sleep, but for daytime rest, giving birth, healing, and dying. Chimps have been observed meticulously gathering the softest leaves to be against their skin. I've always thought the great apes are higher forms of beings than us humans and this bed-making ritual makes me believe I am correct.

I prefer the beginning of the day for making beds. However, this might not be true for some. Making the bed is active. Your blood zooms around, galvanizing the brain. I will admit that I have gotten out of breath just from making beds—especially bunk beds, which are almost impossible to make but totally worth it for whoever is up there at night. I tend to come up with good ideas while I make the bed. Sometimes it's about what I will bring to the school potluck, but often, bigger ideas strike me, like how to apologize to a friend, or I'll think of a good romantic setup. Accomplishment is a part of control, and control a part of cozy, so thematically it falls into place. It's not an insignificant amount of time; it is a legitimate way of stealing time for yourself as, after all, bed making is seen by most as a good habit.

As you make your bed, it's impossible not to feel gratitude for having a place to sleep at all. Pulling and tugging sheets, you're connected to the nest you have given yourself. I suppose this falls under the category of "self-care," which seems to be a trendy phrase, but hurrah for that—self-care is something one can do to make life easier. When you make the bed, you are tending to it—you aren't ignoring it. Sleep is arguably the most vulnerable thing we do during the day, and the most important. In making the bed, we are actually protecting ourselves, and symbolically making sure we are secure, clean, and looked after.

If you share a bed, there are few things better than making it together. Like many people, I am paired up with a busy person who multitasks and is on a smartphone quite a bit. But there is rarely a time when I am making our bed that he doesn't offer to help. Now, because I am controlling by nature, making the bed by myself is sometimes my inclination, but I always take him up on the offer because I have had some of the most meaningful talks with my husband when making our bed together. You can't really do anything else with all those blankets flying around. No spare hands for phones, computers, or the newspaper. It's found time for us to chat about something funny a kid said, or agree that we probably should figure out a date to have dinner with the friends who live just far enough away we have to make an effort to see them. We've even sorted out disagreements. I don't have to be a therapist to say that coziness is often achieved by good communication, and sometimes the most seemingly tough decisions can be satisfyingly resolved in the time it takes to make the bed.

On an almost-three-hour foray on the Internet into making beds, I came across a website called Old and Interesting, a history of domestic paraphernalia. There I found a list of everything having to do with making the bed in Tudor England. Terminology, fabrics, downs, woodwork, and methods to make Martha Stewart squeal with delight—but here are the highlights:

- Joined bedstead—all-wooden bedstead

- Corded or rope bedstead—ropes supporting the mattress instead of wooden slats

- Truckle bed or trundle bed—low movable bed hidden away during the day

- Trussing-bed—bed which can be taken apart, tied up, and transported

- Tester and celure—both words can describe the canopy. Some people use tester to mean the rigid wooden frame or metal rods supporting the draped canopy and think of the fabric as celure. But the distinction is not clear-cut; one inventory in the sixteenth century refers to a "tester of damask." "Tester" comes from the French word for "head," and "celure" has the same roots as the word "ceiling."

- Costers—hangings for the lower sides of the bed, valance

- Dosser—hanging at the back of the bed

- Transom—fabric stretched across the head of the bed

- Pallet, palliasse, paillasse, chaff bed—straw-filled (or chaff-filled) mattress

- Tick—cloth bag and mattress cover

- Featherbed—a "quilt" fabric bag (tick) filled with feathers, often accompanied by a matching bolster;

- Bolster—a cylinder of stuffed fabric, filled with feathers or flock or wool; stretched the whole width of the bed and covered by the lower sheet

- Pillow bere—pillow cover or pillowcase (pillow-bearer)

- Cod—northern English pillow or cushion (also Scottish)

- Happing—coverlet of lesser quality

- Coverture—coverlet, bedspread

- Quilt—either a feather or wool quilt used as a mattress, or a coverlet filled with wool

- Tartarine—"Chinese" silk from Tartary

- Sendal—thick silk

- Samite—rich silk, sometimes with gold threads woven through

- Damask—silk with woven designs

- Chamlet, camlet—a luxury fabric—the name often applies to a mixed weave of silk and animal hair or wool

- Sarsenet, sarcenet—fine, soft silk

- Arras—rich tapestry or hanging made of tapestry

- Say—fine serge, wool, or wool and silk

- Dornick—various blends and weaves in the style of Flemish Tournai (Doornik) fabric, used for hangings or covers

- Baudekin—brocade or other thick silk with designs on it

- Vair—squirrel fur

- Miniver—white fur

- Rennes, Reynes linen—the finest linen sheeting as woven in Rennes in Brittany

- Carde—fabric used for hangings, probably linen

- Fustian—coarse linen cloth (or cloth made from cotton and flax)

- Dowlas—coarse linen used for sheets

- Canvas—coarse cloth, could be used for sheets, or underneath mattress or featherbed

- Worsted—cloth made from wool spun with a firm twist

- Harden, hurden, hardine—rough hemp or linen cloth (made from hurds, oakum, tow)
- Flock—clumps of wool—later also scraps of cloth

Plumping and Weight

PLUMPING IS ESSENTIAL to a cozy bed (or sofa). After years of smacking and whacking pillows unsatisfactorily on top of the bed, I was saved by my friend Maldwin. Maldwin's grandmother taught him how to plump pillows, he taught me, and I will now teach you because it's one of the best things I have ever learned. Hold the pillow with two hands high up above the floor, and then ceremoniously let go and wait for the satisfying sound of it thudding on the floor. Pick it up, turn it around, and drop it again. The result is a perfectly plumped pillow.

As with all things cozy, arranging the bed will be particular to you. How many pillows? Quilts or comforters? Colored sheets or pristine white? I'm particularly sensitive to how heavy the duvet feels. I feel taken care of if something is weighty on me. You know those protective blankets made of lead they put on you when you get your teeth X-rayed? I would like to sleep with one of those as a cover. Studies in occupational therapy have shown that weighted blankets cause the brain to release serotonin and dopamine, which could explain the cozy feeling. In occupational therapy, the term is "deep pressure therapy," and it helps calm. This is probably a reason Beanie Babies are so awesome. Recently, and fabulously, I discovered that people have invented something called a weighted blanket. At first, these blankets were used to help kids with ADHD, but now they are being marketed for everyone and anyone as they help with anxiety, insomnia, and, in my world, coziness. There are those who prefer lightness and simplicity. I wonder if that is because of temperature . . . levity? Some people run hot, and have no trouble falling asleep.

In 1983, when I was thirteen, a TV movie called *The Day After* aired on ABC. It was hugely anticipated, and it was about nuclear war. Everyone was talking about it. It ended up being the most watched TV movie of all time, and it was terrifying (I could have used a weighted blanket to sleep under when I went to bed that night). I don't remember many of the specifics anymore, but there's one scene—I recall it being at the end, but it might not have been—that has always been burned on my brain: There is a woman in her house. Outside the window, miles away, a nuclear mushroom cloud is rising, billowing, and expanding.

Doom is guaranteed. The woman's gaze turns away from the unimaginable, and she begins to methodically *make the bed*. Now, not even at age thirteen did I think, *Death is literally at your door—who cares about making the bed?* As a matter of fact, it made perfect sense to me. In the face of uncertainty, what's better than to do something familiar? To grasp a shred of control, and connect with the place we rest, read, make babies, heal, and sometimes die?

THE BATH

❧

"There must be quite a few things a hot bath won't cure, but I
don't know many of them."

—SYLVIA PLATH

TUB, SOAP, SOAK, sink, warm, tap . . . Writing about this
subject feels like hallowed ground, as if I were writing about a first kiss or my mother's handwriting—will
the words do the job? No matter, I shall plunge in. A fixed
compass to coziness is a bath—even the words surrounding
bathing are good.

"Go to the water!" Julie, a childhood friend, bellowed
the minute I told her I was writing about the bath. "Go to
the water" was something Mrs. Harding, the head of our
elementary school, strongly advised. She was directing our
seven-, eight-, and nine-year-old selves to take a bath—not
to get clean, although that was a perk, but to find calm and
to restore.

Baths are ordinary. They are funny. What's more amusing than a basin you sit and steep in? Millions of children
are routinely plopped into the tub, a kitchen sink, a tide
pool—something with water in it. If ever there was any

trouble in our lives, from a failed test to a broken heart, the very first thing my mother told us to do was take a bath before she uttered another word of advice. You're cold? Take a bath. Someone spoke behind your back? Let me get the water running. Didn't get the job at the video store? Get thee to the tub! Baths aren't really for problem solving—walks and drives are what's needed there. Baths are for restoring, healing, preparing, and resting. Sometimes their purpose is when life has very few other answers, like heartbreak, friend-yuck (a wonderful term a pal coined; can't think of anything better to describe awkward friend messes), sibling rivalry, a dumb cold, job confusion, anger, missing someone, useless jealousy, useless regret, a hangover, FOMO, a long day, nervousness, hurt feelings, a bad meal.

*   *   *

AT AGE TWENTY-TWO, I was terribly heartbroken—distraught beyond my comprehension. I did find the strength to call my dearest friend Miles to cry and *cry* to. Miles listened, but before long he sighed and said, "Well, come on over." When I arrived on his East Village doorstep looking like Courtney Love (it was the '90s) with tears still rolling down my face, he turned me around by the shoulders and marched me straight to his bathroom. Miles, being Southern, gay, and on his way to becoming one of the great American designers, had a bathroom that didn't remotely resemble the bathroom of the scruffy boy who had just dumped me. It looked like something out of a Coco Chanel fantasy. To my knowledge, he had the only oversized marble tub in the Bowery. There were chunky candles perched and glowing from most surfaces, gardenias floating in silver cups, and the steam coming off the rushing tap gave off a heady Victorian bouquet. The heaviest cut-crystal ashtray and a fresh pack of cigarettes sat on a little mirrored table to the side of the tub, in case I really wanted to get my Frances Farmer on. "Plunk yourself on in, darlin', and finish crying. Dinner and a big ol' glass of wine will be ready when you're out." Nothing would mend that heart of mine but time; however, if there is anything cozier than a friend drawing you a bath in a minor crisis, I can't think of it.

Thematically, temperature and control bond baths to coziness. In *Farmer Boy*, there are multiple scenes where the children splash around in baths in a copper basin next to the stove while multitasking Ma makes a supper of corn bread, bacon, and baked apples from scratch.

Taking a bath is respite from the day. It's a pause, a mediation—but also, there is *water*. There is scientific research that says soaking in warm water, especially filled with certain minerals with healing properties like magnesium, calcium, sulfate, and iron, has actual health benefits. It's said to increase circulation, help with sleeping, and boost the immune system. Enriched water may soothe skin conditions, lower blood pressure, and ease sore joints and muscles. A drop or two of essential oils can transform your mood.

When I was small, the rush of cold or hot New York City water coming out of the tap was somewhat of a miracle to me. I remember being amazed at my good fortune that I could put my little mouth under the spout and drink as much as I wanted—for free. There's something about water, right? The mighty oceans, brooks, soupy ponds—we humans love it. It's life-giving—literally; all of us crawled out of it. Being submerged in water is like playing in a galaxy of stars.

We are told our whole lives long to take care of ourselves. That's even how we bid each other goodbye: "Take care now!" But do we always do that? We overwork, deprive ourselves of sleep, eat poorly, beat ourselves up, get into fights, drink too much, and generally run ragged, so if we pause to do something small like take a bath, somewhere inside we must feel that we are following the directions of our doctors, teachers, parents—all the superegos of society, and following directions can be very cozy.

✦ ✦ ✦

BATHS NEED PREPARATION and organizing. Even the hastiest dunks require some consideration; you must think about what you or someone else may need. Is a towel ready when you get out? Will you have music? Will you read? Will you light a candle or sprinkle fragrance like pine or sandalwood under the spout? The smell of your local tap water is sometimes the most comforting. If you are very lucky, you might have a window in the bathroom. Will you open it or close it? There is a lot to adjust in a tub. Having control of temperature is quite formidable when you think about how few things we can control. As a child, when I bathed with my brother, I distinctly remember thinking that I had enormous power and standing because I sat at the front of the tub near the faucets and he sat in the back. It felt like driving a car. I could take the experience wherever I wanted.

If I was too hot, I could grasp the cool metal fixture and let the icy water do its magic. And conversely, even as an adult, I find adding more hot water is one of life's greatest luxuries; you might even turn the knob with your toe.

Will you take an indulgent full tub or a shallow one before darting to the movies?

A lot of the time you are alone, but sometimes there is an opportunity to take a bath with someone else. A pediatrician only had to tell me *once* that it was beneficial for infants to have skin-to-skin contact and taking a bath together would be healthy both mentally and physically. Motherhood, which sometimes is so hard for me, seemed easy as pie if I could do it in and around the bath. If everyone doesn't mind getting pruned, you can spend the entire "witching hour" with your babies drawing soap dragons by running your fingers through the milky surface of tub water.

Of course, baths with a lover are romantic, sexy, and cozy combined—for the most part. But taking a bath alone is what I do most often. I have read some unfortunate articles about baths drying out one's skin, but I choose (from a beauty perspective probably unwisely) to turn a blind, wrinkly eye. I'm in a tub twice a day for sure, and in cold or upsetting times that number increases. In my middle age, I have taken to spooning a few glops of coconut oil into the water, especially if I choose to read, talk on the telephone, or meditate.

HERE ARE THINGS TO PUT IN YOUR BATH:

Sprigs of rosemary. Rosemary is so strong and healing. It feels quite cool to be the kind of person who thinks while they are cooking, *Hey, I'm going to save some of these herbs for my bath tonight.*

Epsom salts. Very effective for sore and strained muscles—maybe aging in general. You can keep them in a big Ball jar in the bathroom. Pretty to look at.

Coconut oil. I like to keep a big tub of the solid variety (gotten at the grocery store) close to the bath so during longer soaks I might rub a scoop into my legs and arms. The warmed oil slides into the water and softens everything up. Emu oil works too.

Oatmeal. Soothing and messy. If you have a rash of any kind, oatmeal is very useful. Rashes make one think of giving up, they are so hateful and aggravating, and oatmeal is a natural salve for a rash and also a natural go-to if one feels like throwing in the towel. Oatmeal is the equivalent of sweatpants.

Bubble bath. Skin drying is a real side effect here, so maybe use only once a week—for elementary-aged children one can be more generous. My brother and I used to pour dishwashing liquid in our tub, creating MOUNTAINS of bubbles that went halfway up the green tile, and both of us have perfectly all right skin now.

White and cider vinegars. Cleans beautifully, and the simple Heinz bottle looks attractive next to the Ball jar of bath salts. All you need is a slosh to have its cleaning properties do some good for your body.

Tea tree oil. Instant spa. If you take a washcloth, soak it with very cold water in the sink, squeeze the water out, sprinkle a few drops of tea tree oil on it, and fold the cloth in half and then in half again, you can rest it over your eyes or on your chest.

Any essential oil. Sandalwood, rose, pine, jasmine—there are millions, and you need only a droplet to transform a mood.

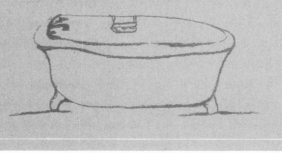

THE KITCHEN

❧

OH, THE KITCHEN! You probably don't need me to tell you kitchens are cozy, but it bears repeating. Kitchens are the central nervous system of a house. They are strong, vibrant rooms of creativity—usually warm, colorful, and fragrant. There are some minimal and sterile, and some overcrowded with oils dating back to the seventies with grubby stoves—but usually all of the senses are in fifth gear in a kitchen. One finds oneself in the kitchen to seek comfort, to be fed, to have a conversation, maybe to warm up—some lucky ducks have a fireplace in theirs (not in mine, but what a great dream that is)—and there's usually a chair for a rest. I'm in the kitchen at least fifteen times a day, mostly to cook. I stuck a banana bread in the oven before I sat down to write this chapter. Kitchens are hubs. And all of the themes of cozy are alive in any one I have ever been in. Ovens, gas flames, boiling, steaming—heat is central to a functioning kitchen.

The clunky, push-button telephone I spent every waking hour on growing up in our Upper West Side apartment was mounted on the wall above the kitchen counter, its long, curlicue cord hanging down all the way to the floor.

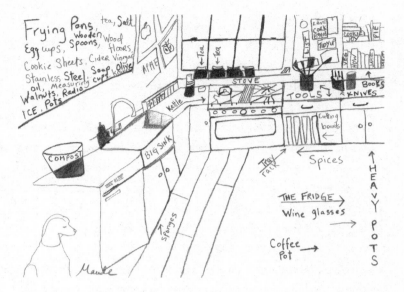

As a teenager, I sat by the phone on a high stool that was painted a French blue, waiting for it to ring. Most of the time my mother would be cooking. I would chat with her and watch her chop onions, brown stew meat in a gigantic orange Le Creuset, or peel vegetables. Inevitably, she would say something like "Would you just look at this," holding up an asparagus stalk. "Look how funny he is, standing up so straight." (She always personifies food things.) And then she would either snap off a bite or toss it in the pan. "You can't cook them for more than a minute," she would say, peering into the steam, "or they turn dull brown and horrible, but if you catch them at the right time . . ." And suddenly Mum would grab on to the handle, pivot, and dump the boiling water into a colander in the sink, dodging billowing steam. "They are the most *MARVELOUS* of vegetables—some people don't like asparagus, but I do."

Kitchens are *intensely* personal spaces. Cooking in someone's kitchen (especially without asking) would be like playing someone else's guitar: you can do it, of course, but be ready to feel the choices, particularities, and, I'll just say it, soul of another while you do. The linoleum floors in some kitchens hold as much meaning as family albums. Generations have trod on them, swept them up, and stood waiting for water to boil. My mother used to lie on the floor of the kitchen when things had gotten too hectic and she needed a reset. There are little nicks and scratches in kitchen counters that have as much meaning as a wedding ring.

WHEN YOU COOK in a kitchen, you invite the outside world and elements to work with you: the sink draws in water, small fire peeks out of the burner, the butcher you got the meat from is with you as you open the brown paper package it came in, the fishmonger's words about the snapper swirl as you broil, the time of day plays a part, seasons, the sea, the language of a recipe, the people in your home, and your own quiet thoughts that are allowed to surface while you wait for a cake to bake. Kitchens are as full of stories as anthologies—if spatulas could talk. Some of our family's stories are tacked up on the wall of our kitchen. Here are the posts and messages to myself that are on my corkboard: "Truth, it's more important than ever." The lyrics to the Thanksgiving hymn "We Gather Together," the peace prayer of St. Francis, a *BE STRONG* decal, a button that says, *I AM A NEWMAN-TARIAN*, a postcard of a donkey, a picture of my oldest son with my brother's greyhound, Oz, and an all-important note to the kids on how to clean up: *1) TURN OFF ALL*

APPLIANCES 2) PUT FOOD AWAY 3) CLEAN DIRTY DISHES 4) WIPE DOWN COUNTERS 5) DOES THE KITCHEN LOOK TIDY?

I can't get enough of corkboards. They allow you to keep things you feel attached to but have nowhere to put—lots of people would say to toss the theater ticket stub you find in your pocket; I say keep it, but stick it on a corkboard. If a kid leaves me a note (rare because of those phones—but it happens), I'll put it on the kitchen corkboard, and later, maybe months later when I look up from chopping, I see their handwriting, and then I think of them, and who they are, and how they have grown from when the note was written. If they are far away, I feel close—and then go back to chopping. The note could remain on the board in my kitchen for a decade.

Even the noises of the kitchen are worth listening for. My mother's timer that's melted on one side ticks so loudly the dogs' ears perk up when I set it. The radio tells us the sports scores and weather reports, music of all genres blasts, microwaves beep, the oven hums, dish soap farts at the end of the bottle, the fridge door sucks as it closes, toasters ding, dry macaroni scrapes as it slides out of the cardboard box, coffee grinders make the loudest sound I have ever heard. That sound used to remind me of my mother; now it reminds me of my husband.

DECORATING

❧

"Anything with a lid makes me want to have a nervous
breakdown, it's so cozy."

—NATHAN TURNER

W HILE RESEARCHING THIS book, I took a trip to San
Francisco. Besides climbing the steep hills and eating wedges of sourdough bread, I went on a tour of the in-
famous prison that sits on an island in the bay; renowned for
some of the murderous inmates it housed, it is now a national
park. Alcatraz is stunningly beautiful, which is a little bizarre
because you can't help but look out from the *jail* and think,
This is a way better view than I have in my hotel—by far. But, of
course, crime and punishment was a misery, and that reality
doesn't leave you while you are there.

It felt eerie to be tourists in our modern sneakers and
backpacks, listening to Patrick Mahoney, a real prison
guard, narrate the audio guide. Maybe it was because of
that feeling that I really appreciated learning that if the inmates living on "The Rock" had good behavior for long
enough, they were allowed to keep the carefully collected
and arranged possessions they had on a little shelf. There
were drawings (many of their own creation) and postcards
on the walls. Some learned to crochet; others had a few

books. While I walked through the chilly corridors, passing cell after five-by-eleven-foot cell, I thought how impossibly difficult it must have been to keep hope alive when you were imprisoned on Alcatraz. How did they do it? Faith? Visitors? A daily exchange with a guard? Meals? Was there no hope? But the small decorative attempts I saw were evidence of optimism and courage.

If we are lucky, we have the freedom and the ability to express it. We are lucky if we have a home to build collections, pin up postcards, and paint walls whatever colors we choose. Even the choice of where to put a single chair can empower and have impact on our daily happiness. I don't even like decorating so much, but I do like noticing what parts of the apartment my family gravitates to and then enhancing those natural gathering spots with paintings of birds on the walls or a place to rest one's feet, and I certainly love a chintz.

My oldest son is a heat-seeker. As a small child, he would find the hot water pipe or heater in any of the numerous places we lived (his father is a professor and we moved around a lot). He would wedge his reedy four-year-old body next to a piece of furniture near the heat source, and wrap himself around the hot-ish pipe like a little sloth. Eventually, after I was remarried, our family settled permanently, and as night follows day, Hugh found his way to the portly prewar accordion radiator in the living room. The only thing that seemed logical for me to do, so he wasn't always on the floor, was build a cozy nook for him there.

We pushed a wide ottoman into the corner between the radiator and a side table with a lamp and the window—

plenty of natural and incandescent light. I gave him a large, sturdy pillow with an owl on it so he could sit up and lean against the wall to read or be on a computer. For years, he practically lived in that spot with his socked feet rammed up against the furnace. He always said it was cozy. Watching him there, giving him that space to be at home, made *me* feel cozy too.

Our spaces are a blank canvas for us to express our personal experience and identity. This is where you have to put on your thinking cap and open your eyes. What are you interested in? What do you love? Who do you love? Where are you from? I live in New York City. Once, at a flea market, I spotted four ratty, inexpensive prints of apples. I thought to myself, *If I frame those and put them in my kitchen, every time I look at them I will know that I'm a New York girl*. I did frame those prints, and I swear that every time I look at them I know who I am. But I'm no designer. Nora Ephron wrote in her movie *When Harry Met Sally*, "Everyone thinks they have good taste and a sense of humor but they couldn't possibly all have good taste." I don't think I have good taste, or a particularly good sense of humor, and that's okay. I know a few things.

If I had to choose one design move to make a room cozy, it would be lamps. Having light distributed all over a room in individual pools gives people choices of where to settle in. Well-placed lamps next to chairs for reading and on tables in dim corners is my cozy go-to. It's not just the warm light, helping you see better—it's turning them all on and off. There is a moment of solitude, which can feel dark when one sits down to work—but if there is a lamp, in a single, thoughtful gesture you can turn a switch, hear the pleasing click, and everything you need to do is illuminated. My body relaxes when the desk lamp turns on, even if I'm looking at a pile of bills.

I have a hard time choosing the right colors—I know I love yellow in a room, but there are so many yellows, it's overwhelming. I also don't have an eye for space. An architect was over for dinner, and she said, "You know, if you turn this table around and push it two feet over so it hits the wall, this area will work for you, not against you." I had no idea what she meant (isn't space just, well, space?!), but I immediately followed her free, sage advice and in two shakes of a lamb's tail turned a space where nobody had ever felt good—or hung out—into one of the coziest spaces in our apartment. Perhaps because the table is against a wall now, we feel more grounded. The room looks and feels comprehensive.

There are people who are born with an innate feel for where objects should go and where drawings should be hung, and have the same instinct about color as migrating birds who know where to fly—they just know. Having an eye and sense of place is like having a beautiful voice or being a fast runner; it's God given. Some make it their profession; some don't.

Because it's such a wide subject, I'm going to ask people I think have a knack for decorating and design to put in their two cents about what they find cozy. My editor would love me to work all of these words of wisdom into an all-inclusive chapter, but I am going to stick to my guns here and just quote these designers, as one of my cozy rules is, if you don't know what you are doing, ask a professional and do what they say. Seeking the wisdom of smarter and talented people has helped me. My father calls something like this "tips from the top."

COZY DESIGN TIPS

**Linda, my mother (not a designer,
but I generally do what she says):**

Small dining tables—round (ours is forty-three inches
in diameter, best for two to four people, can fit six)

Small dining tables—rectangular (ours is seventy-
five by thirty-three, best for four to six people,
can fit ten)

Pillows of just about any size or shape—down, if
possible

Bookcases—in just about every room

Surfaces—not hard (as in marble, tile)

Stools and small chairs—Have a small chair in your
house or apartment. Any four-year-old who comes
to visit will make a beeline straight to it and sit
happily, feeling paid attention to while the grown-
ups do what they do. And stools. Wonderful to
have something to put one's feet on.

Kitchens—not too big

Nathan Turner

NATHAN TURNER IS an entertaining design and food virtuoso.
He's written beautiful books and owns a shop in California
that has a full kitchen right in it so he can entertain! Here is

an example of a childhood feeling and formative emotional attachment informing not only Nathan's personal aesthetic but the way he works.

"The color blue. To me the coziest blue is a deep navy blue that you see in Northern California and Maine. The house I grew up in looked out on a strait that came out of the ocean; it curved and bent. And that color blue—it wasn't that you wanted to jump in it, you wanted to get into a good chair and look at it. And then every night the fog would roll in like a blanket and that meant it was time to go to sleep. Those colors of dark blues, grays, and greens, because of the rolling hills, trigger childhood for me. If color scares you, open the closet and see what the dominant color is, and then go for that. If you are too scared to paint an entire room, just paint the ceiling. Imperfection is cozy. The experience of a room or a dinner party is what you are going for—it's not about creating perfection, that's not the point. People are the point. It's about trying to make people feel good, that's what's cozy."

Eric Hughes

FUN FACT: not only is Eric a prominent designer, but he and Nathan are partners and delight in each other's work as much as they delight in each other. Talking to them at the same time was extremely cozy, because it was fueled by so much love. Love for each other, love for design, love for architecture and spaces, love for food and entertaining, and the earnest desire to help people create all that for themselves. Ah, people in love . . .

"As far as cozy decorating and interiors, what I love is, well, we seem to be going through a moment of self-expression. Socially things don't feel rigid. In this moment there is a certain freedom—and I would venture coziness—in self-expression. How that expresses itself in the home is interesting. There seems to be a genuine appreciation for the handmade, for the odd, for that thing that speaks to you one on one—not mass. And outlets like Etsy and eBay, and in a way Instagram, have really captured that feeling and led the way to a new crafts boom. Who knew thousands of folks whittled handmade wooden spoons? I love wooden spoons—now they are everywhere! Gorgeous pottery—EVERYWHERE!! Macramé—EVERYWHERE. Gorgeous textiles—EVERYWHERE! My point being, this allows us all to bring these moments into our home, these moments of self-expression, these moments of joy—and these moments are cozy and create, especially with time, a cozy home. Through Nathan I've learned there is coziness in organized chaos, in life and in decorating. My interiors used to be highly organized—you might not have thought them particularly cozy . . . over time I've softened my approach and coziness is now a priority. Does love make you a cozier person? In my case, the answer is yes."

Miles Redd

I ALMOST FEEL this is a present for anyone reading. I met and became best friends with Miles Redd in college. He has now, among other things, been named to *Architectural Digest*'s AD 100, a list of "the world's preeminent architects and designers." His massive talent and kindness is clear the second you lay eyes on him; he exudes warmth and style.

1. A huge cozy thing is STRAW, and it comes in a multitude of forms but can do so much in its humble way. It can take the edge off grand, it can give you a fresh-and-sunswept feel, it can be a basket full of logs next to a roaring fire in the country, but it always works and always looks wonderful. Here are some useful ways. On the floor, best way to make a grand English country house feel like you can kick your feet up—I love it wall to wall, but straw area rugs are great too. A straw hat casually tossed on a hook can do a great deal for disguising messy coats usually hanging there as well. Straw wastepaper basket, straw pencil cups, straw chairs . . . use them, paint them (painted straw is wonderful), but it is one of the great decorating tools, and it is *usually* cheap.

2. Trays are essential, and I use them everywhere. They can take a jumble of junk and make it look contained and organized. Just try it. Put a stack of papers in a tray. Voilà— instant organization, but useful in bathrooms to contain the products, wonderful on bars, housing the mixers, in kitchens with oils and vinegars and pepper mills, and of course on desks . . .

3. Pencil cups and paper. I like them tucked in areas, because aren't we always looking for a paper and pen to
   jot something down? Bedside tables, next to phones, in
   kitchens, etc. But get creative with the vessel and the paper and the pen. Nothing uglier than a chipped mug full
   of chewed-off pens. Silver cups with just black flair tips
   are what I favor, but horn cups with number-two pencils
   are also good. Pads of paper that say *DON'T FORGET* is
   a notion borrowed from Albert Hadley, but one I encour-
   age you to steal.

4. Dimmers are also the key to cozy. Lighting, in fact, is *essential*. Lots of sources of light . . . lamps, task, picture
   light, all on about thirty-watt bulbs, will make your house
   glow like a pumpkin at Halloween.

5. Bars—instant cozy. Set a drinks table up in your living
   room, put a tray, ice bucket, bottle of liquor, a small cutting board—and it immediately makes a space inviting.

Vanessa Gillespie

A JEWELRY DESIGNER by trade, Vanessa taught me about the
coziness of working at home while we lived together in the
West Village almost twenty-five years ago. She would sit at
a little work desk with her tools, and carve wax for rings.
Vanessa often had a hand-painted Italian ceramic cup of
cappuccino—half-caffeinated, half-decaf—that she brewed
herself in our closet-sized kitchen. The kitchen, next door to
her jewelry-making corner, could fit barely two people in it
at one time but had a window that looked at the clock tower
of the Jefferson Market Library.

Ness's advice: "If possible, try to have a blanket in every room."

With the advent of the light, versatile, inexpensive, almost mystical microfiber, snug blankets tucked away in any corner is a real possibility.

Katie Brown

WHEN I FIRST got to know Katie—really know her, not just as a lifestyle expert from her books and television shows—she made me these very simple, perfectly weighted, soft, delicious bran muffins. In fact, she kept the batter on hand in her refrigerator so she could make fresh ones for her family or guests at the drop of a hat. Her recipe is in the back of the book. Katie feels like her name, bright and down-to-earth, and she is CO-ZY. Here's why:

> "The thing that I think makes my home the coziest is my attempt to have everything right there, wherever people sit, wherever people sleep, wherever people eat. I want friends and family who come into my home to feel settled and at ease. So I sleep in all bedrooms, I sit in all the chairs and couches and daydream in every nook and cranny. I eat on every table and look out every window so that I can anticipate what people might want when they settle in. The result, I hope, is when you are hungry you grab a snack from the glass canisters I fill for all to see and dig into on my kitchen counter. If you are tired and sleep in our guest bedroom, you have not one, not two, but

three pillows on that bed of varying firmness so you can pick the one that helps you sleep the night away. Want to read a book? Go right ahead because whatever seat you pick will have a light at just the right height for your reading enjoyment. You would like a tea while you read? Not an issue, because there will be a table just close enough for you to rest your beverage on. I want the people I love to want for nothing at any time or any place in my house, because to me that is COZY!"

DOGS AND OTHER ANIMALS

❧

As I have been writing this book, I have turned into sort of a madwoman of cozy. I'm ALWAYS asking myself if the thing I am doing is cozy and why. Washing the dishes: Cozy? Yes, due to the combination of temperature, organization, and control. Delayed airplanes? Well, I'm not going to be idiotic and say that a delayed flight is cozy, BUT, it is what it is, and a delayed flight is a perfect time to make lemonade out of lemons using methods of cozy. Do you like to read? Paperbacks of bestselling books can be found all over airports. You might connect with humanity by people watching. Anyone fighting? Kissing? Eating a burger? Reading a newspaper? Or maybe you would like time alone—the search for a corner where you can enjoy a cup of tea might be the coziest thing you will do all week. Even coming up with an alternative plan can be soothing; there is a satisfaction in making something work. This is cozy. Let's take it to a more difficult degree: the emergency room. Whoosh, this is a tough one. I was in an ER twice in a month. Once by myself in the middle of the night because I thought my appendix was bursting (Peter would have come with me, but I didn't want the teenagers to wake up to a no-parent household; as grown up as teenagers *seem* to be, they really are kiddos). Turns out one's appendix is on the other side of the body. It was probably a kidney stone, but I still was in the ER for a good three hours. Up on 168th Street at two thirty a.m., I had to really search for cozy. It was cold, it was scary, and there were people in dire straits. So how did I find it? First, I watched the nurses at the nurses' station. They have an entire world going on behind those huge U-like desks. Through a level-seven pain, I eavesdropped on conversations. The nurses were gossiping—the universal tendency to talk about others. This made me feel connected to them, which made me think they could help me, which was soothing. The doctors passing by were wearing soft-looking scrubs. I imagined how many times they must go through the wash, how many other people needed their help. This made me feel less alone. I sat in a corner—always a cozy plan for me. Someone brought their pregnant wife a sandwich and chips, which gave me faith in humanity, because I pictured the person in the deli making the sandwich. Even if people are unaware of it, they are helping one another. This gave me hope. The takeaway here is that tuning in—connecting to what's going on around you—is how you get cozy.

Animals are tuned in ALL THE TIME.

This might fall under the umbrella of Too Much Information, but deep in the middle of the other night, I unceremoniously threw up, out of nowhere—must have been something I ate. Anyway, we can all agree it's an unsettling experience. As I lay back down, hair still in a ponytail, damp from washing up, feeling ill and breathing heavily, I wondered to myself, *What on earth is cozy about this? How do people who feel like this all the time get cozy?* I rubbed my feet together, thought about the children, thought about my husband, who was across the country, worried about why I had thrown up—was it the crab cake? Or could I be sick? Cozy wasn't finding me, and I wasn't finding it, and then, as if she knew, my thirty-pound hippopotamus of a dog, Maude, galumphed over so that her back was up against mine. Contact. I thanked everything for her.

When dogs settle, they sometimes take a big deep breath in and let it out accompanied (if you're lucky) with a guttural hum. Feeling the heft of Maude against me, I took a page from the canine book and drew a deep breath in and slowly let it out. Maybe I was sick; maybe all wouldn't be well—but at that moment, the only way I was going to be cozy was accepting the unspoken support Maude was giving me right in that moment. I fell asleep.

This instinctual, loving awareness is why there are service dogs. It's why there is a movie called *Lassie*. It's why, for crying out loud, they say dogs are "man's best friend."

One could write volumes about how cozy animals are—and people have. My pal Julie Klam wrote a deeply beloved book called *You Had Me at Woof*; there's the famous *Marley and Me* by John Grogan—of course, Jane Goodall's *My Life with the Chimpanzees* is astounding. I just read a book called *The Soul of an Octopus* by Sy Montgomery that sort of changed the way I thought about everything. A marine biologist recommended it to Hugh and me when the three of us spent a good forty-five minutes watching a giant Pacific octopus cling to a wall at the Seattle Aquarium.

Here are the coziest animals to me: dogs, gorillas, dragons (mystical, they fly, and I had a beautiful china plate with
dragons on it in my twenties), donkeys (my mother adores
them; they are one of her animals—so compact), pelicans
(nothing in the world is as much fun as watching a pelican
or three plow through the air), parrots (funny creatures—
they eat when the humans do, and they love getting a bath),
blue crabs (spent summers in Maine searching for them all
day; they nestle themselves into rocks and the baby ones are
tiny), panda bears (really, I grew to love them after watching
the movie *Kung Fu Panda*), iguanas (steady creatures), cows
(gentle and lumbering), and elephants (wise, smart, loving
animals). If you choose a few animals in the amazing bio-
diversity to love, they will be touchstones your whole life.
Looking to nature for coziness is a layup.

I saw an exhibition at the Metropolitan Museum of Art
called "The Golden Kingdom." It's an exploration of the
gold work in the ancient Americas—the Aztecs, the In-
cas, and the peoples who came before them from places like
the Andes, Central America, and Mexico. The golden nose
rings, crowns, and mouth coverings could be worn on any
red carpet now, they are so exquisite and fashion forward.
And there are animals on almost every item. One resplendent crown was an octopus, one nosepiece that belonged
to a female ruler from 400 AD had crayfish or shrimp with
jade eyes on either side, and one mouthpiece was a bat. The
explanation of why the craftsmen incorporated animals into
this work, which people wore and would be buried with, is
that animals connected the people to God. Animals were the
pathways to the next phase of life after the physical one they

had just lived. I too believe animals are closer to the spiritual world.

* * *

I JUST FINISHED training a puppy (a second dog), and it's a frustrating, pee-pee-soaked business. Coziness is constantly challenged: you have your life in a routine, your things set up in a pleasing way, rituals in place that support your being cozy in the world, but it all comes crumbling down with a new dog in the mix.

At three a.m. one frigid January morning, while I coaxed Duke around a dirty pile of old snow, anxiously hoping he would connect the elusive dots that "outside" means "toilet," I thought, *Now what in the hell is cozy about this?* I wasn't warm, I was disoriented, and I was alone on the streets of New York—sort of; who knows who might have been lurking around—and then there was HIM: the clueless sniffer. It would take some searching to find the cozy.

Irritated, I looked to the moon to give me guidance. And then, of course, as is so often the case, I thought of *Little House on the Prairie*. Laura Ingalls Wilder wrote a series of books about her and her family's experiences as settlers in the western United States—prairie life. One need only to look to its pages to get set straight. In this case I thought how many chores everyone in every single book does. They milk cows, chop wood, preserve vegetables, sweep out the cabin—you could get eight pages on the mechanics of mending a fence. The careful tending of the house, the earth, and the animals was at the center of their lives. Now, my survival certainly didn't depend on tending to this floppy puppy's needs, but his did.

Thinking about *Little House* brought me right out of my

frustration and gave me a sense of purpose. I marked the clear air and the wonder of the darkness. I thought about who was sleeping and who was awake. Thousands of people in the city tending to something. Maybe a mother was up nursing her baby, or a dishwasher was finishing up in one of the big restaurants, garbage collectors or writers burning the midnight oil. In thinking about the chores of life that everyone has, and the one before me, I was connected to humanity.

CLOTHES

IHATE DISCOMFORT," SAYS Marina Rust, a longtime writer for *Vogue* and one of its style icons. "I moved to L.A. so I didn't have to wear stockings, and by the time I moved back no one was wearing them, thankfully—I loathe binding."

When I think of cozy clothes, I think of comfort like Marina, and not just physical comfort, but cultural comfort, aesthetic comfort, personal comfort. Your body is the first place you start—a localized home that travels through different contexts. Do you have a uniform? What do colors and textures do to your state of mind? I asked my husband what he thought about his suits, and he said they were cozy because they were so reliable—something he can count on like his morning coffee in the mug with the cow on it. He has only a couple of suits; he knows they fit, he knows how they work, he knows what to expect from them.

Fashion seems to be another category; it's just not one I know so much about. For better or worse, when I think about clothes, my mind immediately goes to a pair of navy sweatpants emblazoned with the name of a kid's school running down the leg. Or the faultlessly weighted white cotton bathrobe I am writing in at this very moment—fitted, tidy. My father was forever insisting we all have socks on for warmth. If we were seen slapping around barefooted in drafty March, he would ask, "Where's your socks?" as if we were sitting naked on a pile of gravel. I now find myself looking under tables at my children's feet while they do homework. Do they have socks on? Our French cousins seem to permanently have a scarf or *two* deftly wrapped around them at all times—chic and armed for drafts. I think of the bouncy fleece pullovers I had the children wear in the winter almost every day of elementary school. If I saw those little bodies go out the door donned in fleece, a part of my soul could relax for the entire day knowing that whatever third-grade mountain they had to climb, at least they had a little protection. Prominent on my cozy list are high-top sneakers. I'm not sure I wore any other shoe in my twenties—all mojo was stored in those kicks. Peacoats, decades of blue jeans, and one oatmeal-colored J.Crew sweater I've had since 1986. It strikes me these items are thematically about warmth, and that would make sense as I have spent most of my life in the cooler climates of the northeast of the United States, but at the same time, every fiber in those garments is infused with personal experience. Clothes can connect you with past generations, perhaps to people we never even knew. Lots of times I've complimented a friend on a coat or frock they are wearing that seems particularly suited to them, and not surprisingly the response is, "It was my grandmother's." Think of young lovebirds the world over wearing each other's musty, perfumed, particular T-shirts, or daughters wearing their mothers' wedding dresses. I remember my niece wearing her father's prayer tallit on the day of her bat mitz-vah. Hugh and Thomas have my father's pocket squares in their top drawer awaiting the time of life when they might feel peacock-ish and want to tuck a vibrant piece of silk in a blazer pocket.

My boys, being roughly the same size for most of their lives, had one interchangeable set of clothes, which I only realized when one of them went away for a semester, and we were packing from a single mess of T-shirts. I feel two ways about the one pool of clothes. There is a connected-ness in sharing clothes—"what's mine is yours" is a cozy philosophy—but I have a twinge of regret too as it occurs to me that one's identity can be entwined in clothes. The way a shirt fits could be defining, the particular ink stain on jeans from a pen you were using could be very personal and not easily shared. Is it cozier to have items that are just yours? I can't tell. When my stepdaughter, who falls in between the boys in age, first started spending the night, she wore their clothes too. One set of clothes for three kids.

I've always wished that other cultures' clothes were mine to wear, like the saris of Southeast Asia—there are eighty ways to wrap a sari. Or the North African djellaba, with their huge hoods, which are not only meant to protect one from the sun or keep one warm in the cold temperatures of the mountains, but are big enough to carry a loaf of bread home from the market.

Last year, I traveled with my husband to Marrakech. He had business there. In Morocco, the air was thick with mint; tiny donkeys pulled carts; there were massive jars of olives and pyramids of stacked tagines, Moroccans crowded in the narrow alleyways, and there was a closet-sized shop where one could buy wooden spoons. I luckily found a store filled with colorful kaftans and tunics, some hanging, most folded and stacked in military-like neat piles. I tried on a creamy, woolen djellaba, with silk coffee-colored piping. Looking in the mirror, side to side, I almost felt bridal. The cob, or hood, rested gently on my back, and it did look like I could stick a hunk of bread in there and carry it home. The light, soft robe was elegant, and restful, I wanted to keep it on. I was positive I would wear it all the time at home, especially on cold nights in New York City. But whenever I take it out of my closet, put it on, admire its supple, fine construction, I almost always hang it back up. Somehow it just doesn't feel like my own.

Garments like the djellaba are steeped in tradition and meaning. Even the colors are deeply significant. As objectively cozy as it is, and as beautiful, I feel like a fraud with it on—I don't recognize myself. Perhaps we have to feel that the clothes we wear align with who we are and where we come from. That said, I covet religious habits of all varieties, and I'm far from being a nun. Uniforms, like Peter's suits, are cozy to me, something consistent to be relied upon each day.

Marina also talked about having confidence in who you are with regards to clothes and coziness. She recalled a girl she knew in college who wore a "perfect" shade of red lipstick every day. She was widely admired for it, and people tried to copy her but came up short. "That lipstick was who *she* was, and as much as we all wanted to pull it off too, we couldn't." It's strengthening to have a signature because it's knowable; perhaps it conveys you are familiar with yourself.

But sometimes it's hard to recognize one's clothing identity. Marina told me if you ever get complimented on something you're wearing—run with it! If it's an item of clothing, get as many of them as you can. If it's a color, fill your closet with that color—have it be a signature.

POSTCARDS

◆

POSTCARDS FALL FIRMLY in the personal-experience category of cozy. They are the letter's little brother (or sister—I say "brother" because I have a little brother). Postcards, in their infinite variety, are the easiest, most particular way to quickly check in. *Hello! This is where I am. This is what I did, and I'm thinking about you.* I suppose there is social media or sending a picture on a phone—or even just making a telephone call, but then you don't have the physical object in your hand. You can't see the person's handwriting; you can't carry it around or use it as a bookmark. I've even done that thing where you put on lipstick and kiss the postcard itself to make a *very* personal point. I'm not saying getting a text with a picture of the burrito your friend is about to dive into isn't cozy, but not in the same way as a postcard. Thomas's godmother has sent him a postcard from every place she has ever traveled, whether it be a city close to where she lives or a very faraway land. A lifetime of check-ins. One day he will be blown over by how much she wanted him to know he was in her thoughts.

I'm not sure how long one should really spend in a museum. I'm in the group who ascribe to the go-lots-but-not-for-long way of thinking. The apple doesn't fall far from the tree, because my mother subscribes to this philosophy. In the almost fifty years I've been around, one thing I've learned is that we really do turn into our mothers. Mum thinks that as vastly essential and marvelous as museums are (she majored in art history and worked at the Metropolitan Museum of Art), they can be exhausting, and if you spend too much time in them, you could endanger the impact of what you came to see. This applies the most when you bring children to a museum. It doesn't take long for a child to get a sense of the place and to absorb the contents. Obviously, there will be those who disagree, like Vanessa, who firmly believes a twelve-hour day isn't *enough* time to spend in the galleries of a great museum.

My mother devised something called the Seven-Minute Louvre. Her grandparents lived in France, so the museum she saw the most was the Louvre in Paris, thus the title of the theory, but it applies anywhere, the museum doesn't matter. The Seven-Minute Louvre includes: the *Winged Victory of Samothrace*, the *Venus de Milo*, and the *Mona Lisa*. In seven minutes, you can expose small children to these masterpieces without anyone getting fatigued, cranky, or too hungry. Is there more to see at the Louvre? Resoundingly yes, *but* she didn't want to overwhelm. She wanted us to love museums and perceive them as friendly, easy places where you can be moved to tears, astonished, and transformed. She was teaching us to feel cozy about museums so we would always seek them out for ourselves.

However, art was not the only reason we went to museums—there were also postcards. I vividly remember

Mum slowly walking along the aisle, carefully looking up and down the racks of four-by-six cards with images of famous works like Van Gogh's *Starry Night*, or tiny Egyptian sculptures. Every few cards, something would catch her eye. Maybe it was an image of a donkey (her beloved creature) or a Leonardo. She would pause, lift it up, flip and read the back, and then take four or five before continuing her search. The result of this kind of harvesting is a robust and personal postcard collection—a reservoir, a stockpile for her to draw from and use. A friend of mine gets a postcard from every museum she visits, and instead of saving it to someday give away, on the back of the postcard she writes the name of who she was with and the date, and then sticks it up on her wall.

Postcards are for notes of all kinds, but the great thing about a postcard, as opposed to personal stationery, is that what the image conveys is as important and personal as what you write. Because you have collected the cards yourself, not only is the picture something you particularly like and have chosen, but each postcard has its own history. The recipient might not be aware that you purchased the card they have received when you went on a trip to Dia:Beacon. They are not aware that it was a steamy, beautiful day during the summer, or that you were with your boyfriend—but you know it, and that energy of that day will go into the note you are sending.

Postcards can be sent with abandon. If someone leaves a sweater at your house and you return it the next day, drop it off with a postcard. (If you are lucky, you have one in your collection with an item of clothing on it.) Use one as a thank-you note for dinner or leave one with a plate of cookies on a neighbor's doorstep. Put one in your kid's backpack for acing an exam or send a really jolly postcard to apologize for a missed appointment.

This drawing is of a postcard my mother gave me, and I don't even know how long ago because it has no date, but it's a black-and-white Richard Avedon photograph. It's called *Dovima with Elephants*. Dovima, who was a Dior model, is standing in a black evening gown with a dramatic pale sash, between two great elephants. Her satin shoe is pointing elegantly in the hay on the ground, her arms outstretched between the massive beasts. All at once she looks like a swan, and the elephants look like ballerinas. I am crushed with love for this image. On the back, in my mother's unique (almost illegible) very vertical handwriting, it says, *For my darlingest daughter with so much love from her Mumma.* Simple enough—probably went along with a Christmas present since half of the note was written in red ink and the other half in green. I don't remember the present, but the postcard is everything I love in this life, boiled down to something that cost fifty

cents. It has been leaning against the lamp on my bedside table for countless years. There are pinpricks at its corners that tell me that at one point it must have been tacked on a corkboard.

I have another postcard that lives on my bedside table with a heart at its center. There is one that lives in my kitchen, an Adolf Dehn watercolor of Central Park from a friend who was returning a serving plate. Some I must recycle, but there are ones that I will have for the rest of my life.

Recently our son Thomas was going to a bar mitzvah. He needed a card to go along with the check we were giving the newly minted adult. I sent him to go look in the pile of postcards, and he found a Winslow Homer of two boys sitting in a pasture.

You might consider a postcard a fleeting, isolated object. I like thinking of them, and items of like kind, more like pearls on a long, long-treasured string I carry with me.

RADIO

"... to create a more informed public—one challenged and
invigorated by a deeper understanding and appreciation of events,
ideas, and cultures."

—NATIONAL PUBLIC RADIO MISSION STATEMENT

I'M NOT SURE there are so many radio dials that click anymore
(she wrote, sounding like Grandma Moses), but when they
did, it was a cozy sound—I would even say it triggered a
physical response in me. Like when you take the first drag
of a cigarette, sip of tea, or bite of chocolate, and your blood
vessels widen and dilate—same goes for the radio dial. The
click meant that information was coming your way. Weather,
traffic, news, stories, facts, opinions, all of it was going to be
mainlined into your system. And then there are the people.
There are radio personalities I feel so close to, I would invite them to my children's weddings, and yet I had never met
one—until this year. I had been wanting to write a chapter
on radio because the radio seems like a cozy layup to me—
built-in, free, accessible to most, but what was I going to say,
Listen to the radio, it's cozy? Of course, I wanted to say that,
but who am I? But, if I ever met a radio host . . .

When I say I was starstruck when the bright-eyed woman

(think Julia Roberts) with a good blowout standing next to me was introduced as Rachel Martin, the authoritative voice I hear almost every morning while washing dishes, making tea, and gathering for the day, I mean, it was like 1998, when I ran into Dan Rather at a CBS elevator—I gasped. In Rachel's case, I had to take a seat until I came to my senses. Once I did, I got bold. This was a once-in-a-lifetime chance to ask a professional if what I suspected was true—is radio cozy?

About a week later, Rachel told me on the phone:

"Radio is the most intimate medium. Two voices, no distractions, like makeup, clothes, cameras that distract from the content. There's nothing like the sound of a voice in your ear. I put the earpiece in, and I can feel the person. Intimate communication is deeply comforting. The voice is someone's true self—there's authenticity in it. And I get to be myself, without artifice. When you ask real questions and hear the person pause to truly answer authentically, the audience feels like they are a part of it—and they are. Also, radio is in your personal space, your kitchen, your car, the shower, and I think that makes people feel close to you as host, the guests, and the process. Then there is the studio, do you want to hear about my studio? [Um, YES.]

"I am a person who needs and really enjoys the sun and a lot of light, but not in my studio. There we keep the lights really low, so it's a very dark space. I have a fuzzy green blanket my aunt gave to me because it's cold in there. I always have it over my legs. My coffee is always on my right. I take a travel mug from my house to work, and it's just ugly and boring, but I am very attached to it—to the handle. I leave at three in the morning from home, and no matter how hard I try, it's always sort of a disaster, and I'm grumpy, so when I get to the studio, I take pains to make the physical space cozy—make it okay so I can do my job. I have to take some ownership of the world around me. So the font on my screen always has to be Arial fourteen. There has to be order, so the show lineup is always on the left of my screen and the news feeds are on the right, like Twitter, Fox, MSNBC, etc. I wear earphones, and the left headphone is on my ear so I can hear what's on the show, and the right has to be off my ear so I know what's going on in the studio. I can't record anything until it's all arranged. So much about the news is last-minute; it changes rapidly and you can be thrown into a variety of situations that can feel wild—like everything goes out the window. But if the structure I've created is in order, I feel able to do what I have to do."

Bingo. I knew it. Radio is a towering club sandwich of cozy. Just click it on.

SEWING

CAN'T SEW OR knit, due to brain wiring, but I know sewing is cozy. I can hook a rug, and I learned to do it years ago when I lived in Maine for a winter. I took an adult education class that was associated with the town's Baptist church sewing circle. The tidy church kitchen where the class met was toasty warm, and smelled like wet duck boots, ironed linen, and coffee. Four or five New Englander women and I sat on cold folding chairs pulled up around a linoleum table. Like the chairs, the women would warm up as the evening progressed, silence turned to a soft hum of chitchat as we braced ourselves gently against the frames, yanking strips of wool through burlap. If I could pick another job, I might be a rug maker.

The Baptist sewing circle I'm talking about is 159 years old. The circle's quilters, sewers, needle pointers, weavers, and knitters (all women) meet once a week in a shingled building that used to be the town's school. Every Tuesday afternoon, the women arrange themselves in front of looms and Singer sewing machines, skillfully making everything from woolen socks to the finest tea towels. From what I've heard—I have never dared step foot in the building, it would feel like marching onto the Senate floor—there are button boxes sorted by every conceivable color and shape; drawers of felts, calicos, and flannels; miles of yarn and thread; and hot coffee brewing to drink with homemade nutty, chewy cookies when it comes time for a break. Its members, a lattice of revered, mostly stoic woman, most of whose families have lived there for more than ten generations, have the aura of tenured professors, so esteemed you dare not speak to them unless addressed.

It feels like a secret society, a private club; however, there is one day when the Sewing Circle puts on a fair in the school gym. It could be my favorite day of the year: the Sewing Circle Fair. After you have gotten pot holders, pincushions (maybe in the shape of a heart, if you please), and if you're lucky, a new hand-cross-stitched apron, there is a table set up with cold ham, egg salad, and cream cheese and chutney sandwiches wrapped in waxed paper. For three dollars, you may choose any sandwich with exactly seven Lay's potato chips on the side, and pour yourself a paper cup full of pink lemonade.

*　*　*

ONE OF OUR boys' grandmothers, Ann, is a member of the sewing circle. I asked her about it. Here's what she said.

> "After I was married, I made draperies for our New York apartment. They covered an entire wall and were lined and interlined and had a Greek key trim. I was pregnant. Later I made outfits for Comer and Ben, but I lost interest in sewing boys' clothes and I soon went back to sewing for myself. I got a Bern-

ina sewing machine and it does make fancy stitches. Nine grandchildren got everything from rompers to Halloween costumes.

"Now as I grow old, I do not sew for grandchildren or myself. We have need for nothing. My machine sits at the ready, however. When it occurred to me to join the Baptist Church sewing circle last summer, I walked in the first day and almost drew a sigh of relief. All of those sewing machines, fabrics of every weight and fiber, trims, patterns, women happily knitting, sewing, embroidering, and chatting quietly. It was sheer heaven to me. I announced to Pat Mitchell, the president, who greeted me, that I could sew, and was there anything for me to do? She put me right to work, and I haven't paused since. I've never once considered the word 'cozy' to describe a Tuesday working in that magical old building, but I guess that's exactly the right word. I always feel at peace there, comfortable."

PART III

NECK OF THE WOODS

IT'S EASY ENOUGH to see how one might find coziness in the bosom of a home, but adjusting yourself to where you work and live as a citizen in your neighborhood is perhaps a more interesting endeavor. Let's widen the view. How wonderful is it to find harbors of cozy in public spaces? We spend most of our lives outside the house, why wait until you get back to the sofa to feel the shiver of well-being?

I fear a bit, as I write this book in a time of turmoil and end-of-days atmosphere, that sturdy outside mainstays like the mailbox won't be around for very much longer. Goodness, that sounds too nostalgic, and really, it's useless to worry about the extinction of the mailbox. But in a time when children are marching in the streets and wars rage on distant shores, isn't it wise, even necessary, perhaps, to take note of and honor things that work and connect us to others or ourselves? To dog-ear parts of the world—water towers, road maps, banisters, community gardens, school offices, food trucks, and train conductors—as things we can depend on to get through?

I've read Richard Scarry's *Busytown* books to the kids a million times. They were about the interworkings of a town—the fire station, a grocery store, I think there was also a hardware store. Any time my mother took *us* to a hardware store, she said, "My, doesn't it smell good in here?" And now I find hardware stores cozy. Just the other day, a hardware store came to my rescue. I had woken up on the wrong side of the bed, hadn't gotten enough hours. It was raining and my driving had been frustrating and jolty. My mood was alienating our family, and I was having a hard time turning my frown upside down. The five of us were in the little town of Belfast, in Maine, and as one does, I shot off on my own to do an errand or two. Once alone, I saw the Home Supply Center on Main Street. I didn't have anything to buy, but I went up the three wooden steps anyway, as I knew the bins of nails, rows of Ball jars, and packages of seeds had the power to turn it around for me. The owner asked if he could help me. "No thanks," I said, taking a deep breath. "I just like the way it feels in here."

"Well, that's something we like to hear," he said. "You can stay as long as you like."

WEATHER

WHEN I STARTED using the weather as a tool for coziness, climate change wasn't a topical issue. A rainy day was an opportunity for reflection, organization inside the home, cooking, reading, doing puzzles, paying bills, responding to letters, raincoats, and puddles to send your kids to jump into—and for a writer, rainy days are a ticket to ride.

Now the weather, once seen as mundane, is political—and, with alarming regularity, dangerous. I don't want to trigger anyone, and I feel that I may. However, weather, no matter who you are or where you live, has a towering, surrounding impact on your day. We all look to the weather—it dictates mood, determines what we wear, what activities we do, how people interact, our perspective, what we eat, how we walk down the street to work. Talking about the weather is a tried-and-true hammock for conversation—one can fall back on it and relax, knowing that everybody will have something to contribute.

Climate is a touchstone. I think of people the world over shuffling to the window first thing to look at the sky. After cold winters, I love how New Yorkers aggressively wear open-toed shoes and shorts on the first warm day of spring.

There is a weather channel! The weather ties us, like when you make eye contact with a stranger as you both try to jump over the same moat-like puddle to cross the street, you almost want to hold hands. My phone displays the weather in all the places where people I love live, and every morning, before I've left the sheets, I scroll through each town to see temperatures and precipitation. Even if I don't speak to the person, I imagine the sweater they will be wearing, wonder if they will go swimming, have a little worry if they might be driving on icy highways.

For me, the words "apparently, it's going to rain all day" convert in my brain to an Emma Thompson–like voice saying, *Don't worry, everything is going to be okay*. Even though all the research I can find says that, scientifically, light and sun make you feel better, the opposite is true for me. I chose to move from California back to New York in the 1990s because of the lack of rainy days; it was never even overcast.

This Sunday morning, it's raining, and for the first time I know of, my husband asked Alexa to play Joni Mitchell. (Alexa is the machine we have in the kitchen—I use it for spelling when I write, *Alexa, how do you spell "psychology"? Alexa, how do you spell "calendar"?* She gets it right every time.) One of our teenage kids got her schoolwork and climbed into the corner of the sofa to read. I just saw her arm float up to switch on the lamp over her head. If it were a sunny day, I would bark at her to go sit at a table to do homework, but since it's raining I let it go—much more engaging to be in the corner when it's gray and wet out. The dogs sleep heavier, the lilies I bought in the middle of the week emit an entrenched, intoxicating fragrance, and the sound of the water hitting the tin roof next door can sometimes be as exciting as Christmas morning. Lots of the coziness comes from being in from out in the rain. "In" is quite a lucky place to be, whether it's your own home, a coffee shop, a classroom, a barn. When you are aware of shelter, there is most often gratitude that comes along with it.

A friend of mine says she finds coziness in Central America. The balmy zephyrs, crashing waves, and canopies of the rain forests are cozy to her. It never occurred to me that tropical climates could be cozy, as I have spent so little time in them, but *of course* they are. This brings me back to the foundation of this book: coziness can't be defined by one standard; it only aligns with what is inside of us. What we know, what we love, what we feel connected to and familiar with. Just the other day, I heard a scientist from Antarctica calling into a New York radio station. Naturally he didn't grow up there, but has worked on the southernmost continent for his adult life. As he described his observations and studies of the tundra's dry winds and deafening cold, it sounded like he was describing the coziest place on earth—Antarctica! When you feel emotion and sense of place from someone, it's because they believe it.

* * *

IT'S THE PITS writing about singing in the rain or walking in sunshine when the climate has been so hard on the world. Or how hard we humans have been on the climate. I want to write about scurrying arm in arm with a pal under an umbrella, but flooding, fires, winds, and soaring or plummeting temperatures the globe over have destroyed so many lives, it's hard to.

But perhaps the connections made during extreme weather are where the hard-fought coziness is unearthed. Think of the relief work, heroic stories of citizens being clever and brave and doing the right thing. Like the bakers in Houston who got shut in their shop for two days while Hurricane Harvey raged. The bakery was unaffected by water, so the guys, even though they had no idea about their own safety, or the safety of their loved ones and city, had brilliant foresight that food would be needed, and what did they have? Flour and ovens. They got to work and baked *bolillos* and *pan dulce*—over five thousand pieces of bread to feed the neighborhood when the storm subsided. There was a businessman, "Mattress Mack," who owns a massive chain of stores in Houston. He opened all of them to victims of the hurricane, and he himself drove the dinosaur-sized trucks used for deliveries to comb the streets looking for people in distress. The managers of his stores gave weary, overextended first responders brand-new, top-of-the-line Tempur-Pedic beds for much-needed collapse and rest.

In the unusually mild autumn New York City had that year, the hurricanes hitting Texas, Florida, Puerto Rico, and the islands of the Caribbean had all of us worried but were far away. I chose to donate money and then cook for my kids, who were starting their school year, and clean closets to ease my fear for our country. On the radio, which was continuously playing, the strongest voices coming through were those of the national guardspeople, firefighters, first responders, government officials, and citizens: "We're all in this together."

NATURE

"One touch of nature makes the whole world kin."

—WILLIAM SHAKESPEARE

IT'S RARE I feel steady and free of worry, so I join countless people and comb the sky, ocean, and trees for good omens. If I come across a pearly green luna moth clutching a screen door in Maine, a red-tailed hawk flying over the buildings of the Upper West Side, a silver fox slinking across the road in upstate New York, I interpret these marvelous chance sightings as indications all will be well. Maybe it's a way to have

control in a chaotic world. Maybe when you feel worried, about something like getting a job, there is a pit of uncertainty that is difficult to fill. Perhaps I should have a better meditation practice to handle concern. I don't know, but if catching a leaf in the air as it falls from a tree makes me feel cozy *and* that the kids will pass their exams, I'll take it.

The person who spends the most time in nature in our family is our oldest child, Hugh. When I was approaching this section of the book, he had just come home from tromping through the backcountry of Alaska, and was loitering around the house all tan and scraped up. An astounding realization for me as a parent is that when a kid speaks about something they have discovered and taken interest in on their own, it's better than watching them take their first steps. For a teenager who seems to want less and less to do with me, Hugh really wanted to talk with me about Alaska. It seemed that the entire state was cozy to him.

"I *thought* seeing a moose in the wilderness would be cozy, but actually it was eerie and menacing. Moose are enormous, first of all—seeing a two-ton behemoth of a creature standing one hundred feet away from you will give you chills—it shocks you, suddenly all the real stories of how dangerous moose can be surround you. You're in awe, but you're frightened. On the other hand, when I saw three grizzly bears up close (they were in the bushes about ten yards away), there was coziness because I could see my own family in them. Bears are so human—you can recognize every emotion in a bear. What we find cozy is what is familiar, so when you're in the wilderness, especially for me because I live in a city, it's like being in outer space—so different . . . but seeing emotions I could spot in a *bear* was surprisingly cozy—and bears were by far the animal we were most warned about."

"Inside every animal is an individual
with its own emotions and needs."
—*NATIONAL GEOGRAPHIC* PHOTOGRAPHER

I'm a city dweller. I don't spend a lot of time in deserts and mountains, but I do love reading *National Geographic* magazine. I hit up their Instagram daily. In the 1970s, most families I knew had collections of *NatGeo*s in their rec rooms and bathrooms. All the school libraries I've ever spent an afternoon in had the most recent issue prominently displayed, and if you wanted, there were rows and rows of the iconic bindings waiting for you to use for a research paper. In the technological era, *National Geographic* has eighty-five million Instagram followers. In 2017, they gained seventeen million followers and had 6.1 million comments and 1.4 billion likes. That feels universal to me. Do we all love it so much because we see ourselves in these creatures? Do we connect to them in a different way than we connect to one another? Is it easier to find comfort in trees and mountain ranges and the animal kingdom? If so, then we must look to it for comfort and solidarity, and we must protect it.

Hugh, just like all of us, struggles with this and that, and that worries me—but on that trip to Alaska, he found solace and wisdom from the most prickly of creatures.

"Another time I was cozy in the backcountry was every time I saw a porcupine. Sometimes you'd be hiking, and boom, there would be a porcupine just ambling along, minding its own business. It was not only really funny and cute, but it made me think that in life—even in really hard times, like a divorce [he said that—I swear] or death, there is *always* some kind of 'porcupine' walking by minding its business—and taking him in will make you feel better. Even in the most wild and unforgiving environments, the world gives you a porcupine, and that's cozy."

FLOWERS

HOWEVER OLD-FASHIONED AND out-of-touch this sounds now, one of the nicest things anyone ever said to me was, "Isabel, you would be such an easy wife to have—all one needs to do to keep you happy is give you a good meal and fresh flowers." My dear old friend Robert, who was visiting me in college, said it as we were walking through the Village, home to my ground-floor studio on Thompson Street. We had just eaten spaghetti carbonara. Now, we were not in a romantic relationship, nor had either of us been married, so what did he really know? I'm sure my first *and* second husbands would do spit takes and guffaw uproariously at how much more it takes than spaghetti and peonies to get through a marriage with me, but on principle, I think Robert was on to something. Having flowers around you, especially inside, is cozy. Of course, beauty plays a part, but the bigger idea is that even a single daisy stem connects you to the great outdoors.

In the 1980s, there was a rise in Korean delis in New York City. Seemed like there was one on every corner. They were well organized, clean, packed with paper towels and instant coffee. In the middle of it all, there was usually a hot-food buffet with rows of sticky fried drumsticks, bright green stalks of broccoli, and oily glass noodles flecked with red pepper. Outside, big black plastic buckets filled with flowers wrapped around the corner of the store; roses, tulips, hydrangea, sunflowers, bright blue carnations, and curlicue bamboo stems in rows waiting to come home with you. These delis made it possible for a young city girl to bring nature, color, fragrance, and beauty right into the apartment for not *too* much money. And as it happened, there was a particularly great Korean deli right on my corner. Every once in a while, for a treat, I would spring for a bunch of freesia for my bedside table. Well, they would be on the bedside table when I slept, but they would move to the desk while I wrote papers, to the sofa if I was reading, and even the bathroom to take a bath. Flowers don't have to stay in one spot; my friend Bess hauls vases of lilac around with her everywhere she goes in her house. The thinking is lilac blooms for such a short period in the spring, you can't waste a minute while they're available to be in one's home. Some people (like my mother) find it cozy to have a bouquet dependably in the same place, like a Bible in a drawer, or the pair of reading glasses one keeps by the stove. I'm now thinking of all the places my mother keeps a small arrangement of flowers from her garden. The biggest display is on the front hall table; in the summer, this could be black-eyed Susans or cosmos. A very small vase that would fit a child's handful of nasturtiums is always on the 1950s enamel kitchen table, and a nosegay of roses or even a single huge sunflower is next to where my father sits on the sofa. These are her constant floral companions, and if I think of those vases empty I feel heavyhearted.

Flowers are reminders of the great outdoors, of movies and romance. They cheer you up—they are pleasures. They make me feel like I have my act together, that I won't fall off the edge. Flowers aren't only for you, but also for others—they bring happiness so easily. My designer friend Miles says, "Something green or alive is *essential* for a cozy apartment. This can be so simple. Go in the yard and cut one sprig of something, a fern, a magnolia, just a branch with a few green leaves that you like, and stick it in a simple clear bottle. This can be an empty wine bottle (with labels removed, please) and placed on a bar or mantel or hall table. You will be surprised how just something green can warm a space right up."

At my grandmother's funeral, years and years ago, we all read sections of letters she had written. In my piece, she described a vase of lilies on a piano "slurping away thirstily." Her personification of the flower made me think that flowers inside the home were important to her, although she never said that to me, but every time I fill a mason jar with tap water to plunge thirsty daffodils into, I think of her.

It's not easy maintaining plants and flowers in your home. Fresh flowers like to have the water changed every day. Certain plants are easy to kill. If you let the flowers die, well, that can be disheartening. They take some doing, but even if you don't have them around constantly, it's good to keep flowers in mind for certain times. Whenever there is a big snowstorm coming, I make sure to get flowers. Emptying all the vases around the bedrooms and living room, giving them a good scrub, and setting out to the deli is my version of battening down the hatches, controlling what I can't. If the kids have exams, or if I'm on deadline, I think flowers send the message to *keep going*. When anyone comes home from a business trip or a tough time away, I try at least to have daisies on the kitchen table, as they are welcoming. Flowers will aid in healing, I am certain. Most of the time people give flowers when they are being thoughtful and generous, so even if it's one flower in a small cup by a bed, it will be an *aide-mémoire* of those positive human instincts.

Deli Tulips

CREATURES

THE METROPOLITAN MUSEUM OF ART recently had an exhibit of American Indian art borrowed from the Fenimore Art Museum and the Thaw Collection. My son Thomas and I went. One of the artifacts is a very rare club made of bone. On one side of it, the owner had carved a self-portrait, and on the other side of the handle he engraved his guardian spirit, which was a *snapping turtle*. Almost every treasure on display had images of animals uniting the object to its owner, signaling the deep and important bond those cultures had to the natural and animal world.

It's cozy to have an animal that you identify with, and that's why one of the cozier pastimes is sitting around a living room trying to figure out your spirit animal, and even better if it's with a group so you can figure out the spirit animal for everyone you know. I don't have the audacity to compare this game to the sacred vision quests of other cultures, and if it seems like I am, I'm really sorry. It's more that I hope for myself and others that we can find comfort and inspiration in the natural world that is, in fact, so close to us.

I thought I was an elephant for ages, but really I think I'm a grizzly bear, or possibly a she-wolf.

Isabel: Bear	Mo: Swan
Husband Peter: Dolphin	Lindsey: Dog
	Bill: Dog
Hugh: Octopus	Van: Panther
Sage: House cat	Ivy: Owl
Thomas: Elephant	Andrew: Rat
Rudy: Dog	Nonie: Dog
Sasha: Eagle	Doug: Giraffe
DeSales: Crow	Shari: Rooster
Tracy: Wolf	

In the Middle Ages, in order to protect the small city of Siena, Italy, from its enemy Florence, the municipality divided itself into seventeen districts, or *contradas*. Each *contrada* raised money so it could defend the city militarily and represented itself with an animal or symbol from nature: eagle, caterpillar, snail, owl, dragon, giraffe, porcupine, unicorn, she-wolf, seashell, goose, dolphin, pantheress, tortoise, ram, rhino, and elephant. The identification the Sienese people feel for their *contradas* is not unlike how characters in Harry Potter identify with whatever Hogwarts house they belong to. The *contradas* still thrive hundreds of years since their inception, and are a source of deep civic pride. The moment you are born into a *contrada* or become a member later in life, that's *it*. If you are an elephant, you are an elephant, and proud of it—it represents who you are forever. The patron saint of Italy and Europe, St. Catherine, is a goose.

The people of Siena are historically and passionately tied to their districts—deeply loyal and genuinely serious about them. Every important life event, from baptism to marriage, takes place within your *contrada*—and there are rivalries between them! I spoke with Sienese art historian Christina—a caterpillar—about this.

"Each animal has a character, a nature about them," she said. "It is the very center of who you are as a citizen of Siena."

RIVERS

❧

"Black muddy river, roll on forever,
I don't care how deep or wide, if you've got another side,
Roll muddy river, roll muddy river, black muddy river, roll."
JERRY GARCIA AND ROBERT HUNTER

RIVERS ARE DEPENDABLE landmarks of coziness. So much of civilization developed along rivers, they are close to many people. History resides on the banks of them. The Nile, the Amazon, the Mississippi—they are portholes to various classrooms and the teachers who have taken me to their tributaries. Even the word "silt" conjures the smell of chalk and paper, sturdy memories of my fourth-grade peers, heads down, seated at groups of desks, holding pencils, diligently labeling geographical features on mimeographed copies of maps.

For long chunks of my life, I've lived by the mighty Hudson River. The familiarity of its giganticness, the New Yorkers running and biking alongside its banks, the tugboats and barges, its white caps and tales of planes landing on it, all weave into something of a life blanket that I can tuck around me. I should have named a kid or a dog Hudson. I've been looking to it for coziness for so long that even hearing its name included in a morning news story or seeing it in a title of a book adjusts my mojo, makes me feel good, and grounds me in my forty-eight-year sense of place.

Perhaps you drive along a river every day and don't even know that you love it so deeply and connect to the color, smell, or force of it. There is so much nature around us, so many opportunities to see our own reflection—are you walking by it unawares? Is there a river you know? Could you feel attached to it? Why? Is it lazy or rushing? Are there people using it for fishing or playing? Washing clothes? Are there trees lining it, and do you sit under a particular one? Did you have a ravine by your house growing up, so the sound of a river could stir childhood memories that could aid you now?

CIVICS

"When you serve, it doesn't just improve your community; it makes you part of your community. It breaks down walls. It fosters cooperation. And when that happens—when people set aside their differences to work in common effort towards a common good; when they struggle together, and sacrifice together, and learn from one another—all things are possible."

—BARACK OBAMA

PULLING THE LEVER at the polls, sitting in the voir dire awaiting jury selection, marching on Washington— these governmental systems and practices are all cozy to me. I come by the feeling honestly: at age eight, my father made a run for city council in New York City and forty years later is chair of his town's board of selectmen. My parents met while working on a presidential campaign, and we were all encouraged to join our student councils.

Jury duty is a chance to participate in one of our country's most satisfying systems. A lot of people *argue* with this, find it counterintuitive. I will make a case (pun totally intentional). If some themes of cozy are connection, organization, and self-knowledge, in jury duty, we have a perfect storm.

Do you remember standing in line in kindergarten? You had to find your partner, move into your "line spot," listen and pay attention. When I think of the feeling of holding Nina Gould's hand (both of us were *G*s), and looking up to the teacher, who had raised her hand in a peace sign to signal us to be quiet, I get the same feeling as I do in jury duty listening to a judge. When asked by a lawyer if I am able to "come to a decision solely based on the facts of the case and how they align with the law as the judge describes it to you," I am being asked to get specific and real with past experience and consider if I can do the job at hand. In order for our small societies to work, *sometimes*, we must listen and do as we are told.

When my first solicitation for jury duty came in the mail, I was living with my parents. I recall Dad holding the summons like it was a golden ticket from Willy Wonka's chocolate factory and saying, not unlike Leslie Knope from the television show *Parks and Recreation*, "Oh, Ish! Look what came for *you*!" without a shred of sarcasm or irony. What he knew was that I was about to connect with the greater good—to him, there is no higher honor. And all I did to earn this privilege was register to vote.

After serving on a civil case back in 1988 (I have served three times since then—two civil, one criminal. I was an alternate on one of the civils and juror number eight in the criminal, a drug case that was unsettling and sad), I asked the bailiff at 60 Center Street, the New York State Supreme Court, if I could serve on jury duty as a summer job. Of course, he stoically shook his head no, but I was earnest.

How I wish people could share in my feelings that jury duty is one of the coziest experiences we have as Americans. First of all, just like at school, you must be prompt—everyone, some slightly grumbling, gets there at the same time, paper cup of coffee in hand. You and hundreds of members of the community from all walks of life—CEOs to guitar players—file through the metal detectors and proceed to your assigned jury assembly room.

Once you have checked in, there are choices to be made. You can assert control just like you can control the tap water in a bath. Right away, you can pick a seat near a window, or in a corner, or maybe next to someone who looks interesting to talk to—or not, if you prefer to read, fill out a crossword, or get work done while waiting. You may bring a beverage into the room. As it is the morning, most have coffee or tea. In the New York courts, there are vendors supplying drinks and small snacks. I imagine the lawyers know the guy pouring coffee by name. At some point, the clerk will come to the front of the room and call random names. This is an exciting time, as you might hear, "ISABEL GILLIES," and *then* you can go with your group to meet the judge and lawyers who will interview you one by one to see if you are able to be impartial and determine a verdict based solely on what is written in the law.

During this traditional process, even if you aren't aware of it, you are unifying with those around you. You are being shaped by the system into a population that will eventually put their minds together, determine the facts of the case, fairly consider, and come up with a plan of action in accordance with the law. Trust is being handed to you; it's an enormous responsibility, but you are not alone. By the time you and the other members of the jury have sat through the trial and come to a verdict, you are a team. You are bonded forever to a group of people you had never met, and in all likelihood will never meet again. You learn about people's ideals, where they come from, their perspectives, jobs, children, and sometimes even dreams. I wouldn't doubt there are a few who have fallen in love on jury duty. Just underneath the bureaucracy, there is a genuine humanity that you can feel from the moment you walk up the steps and under the Corinthian colonnade.

It's an honor given to us in this country, *and* in New York City, if you deliberate through lunch, a clerk will come and take sandwich orders that will be delivered from a nearby deli. The first time I served on a jury—thirty years ago—I chose to order turkey and Swiss with mayo on a deli roll and chocolate milk. Everyone got exactly what they wanted.

TECHNOLOGY, TWITTER, AND OTHER SOCIAL MEDIA

Loads of mornings I wake up with anxiety. Usually, it's about a kid—"you're only as happy as your least-happy child" is one of my favorite clichés. To ease it, I get straight to the work of cozy. I might make a phone call seeking any advice or help I can get from a friend or parents and apply it to the issue at hand, make tea, make the bed, walk the dogs—maybe meditate, although I'm not as consistent as I would like. I try to listen, perhaps go for a run, work. But the tool that distracts me and makes me feel peaceful when all else fails is Twitter. I have *a lot* of misgivings about social media, and agree with the throngs of experts who believe it's putting us all on the verge of a mental health collapse, but I gotta be real and include it.

We spend a lot of time personalizing our media and technology. I adore my Bitmoji avatar! Is it cozy to see myself as a cartoon? I guess so—kind of reminds me of "Saturday-morning funnies," as my father called animated TV. Sending a Bitmoji to a friend feels more loving, it has a wink, it's something to get a kick out of. I would bet the whole world finds Bitmojis amusing. It makes me feel cozy to feel I'm in on a joke the entire planet thinks is funny.

How many hours have you lost coming up with a ringtone? With all of those choices, every time I end up choosing "CLASSIC" because it sounds like the 1970s when I was a kid. At the moment, I can't think of my kids' ringtones, and I'm appalled to say that's because they don't talk on the phone. Talking on the phone for me is top five on the cozy list, but I suppose not for Gen Z.

Community, connection, and control. The World Wide Web scratches some of the same itches as public transportation. When you log on to Twitter, you are among the endless voices. Idea after idea appears on your little screen, and no matter how we are all trying to say we aren't addicted and attached to it—I mean, I am *forever* bragging that I don't take my phone to the toilet—really, the weighted, hand-sized friend (let's just call it what it is) I am always holding on to is a porthole to a cyberneighborhood that can be as comforting as the one Mr. Rogers used to sing about on PBS. On Twitter, there are people resisting ugly ideologies, sending me recipes, posting crushingly adorable pictures of baby rhinos, highlighting intelligent reporting on everything from elections to face creams. When you are on Twitter, you are not alone! You can tweet out and get reactions in real time—lose yourself in the global community.

I'm not saying it's healthy. There is so much hate and horror on it too, but is there a dialectic there we should at least be aware of? Frankly, smoking was pretty damn cozy when I did it, and it's lethal. Is being addicted cozy? Yikes, and NO, but sort of yes? I'm addicted to watching TV in the evening, I'm addicted to caffeine—people are addicted to running—and almost everyone I know is addicted to social media. There are addictive qualities to community—you've just got to know what's going on, connect, log on, and when you find out, you get a hit. Scientifically, one of the hits, along with dopamine, is oxytocin. This supernova of a hormone is even called "the cuddle chemical," "the love hormone." And "the social hormone." These hormones are powerful, and social media is in bed with them. So, like everything, moderation is something to keep very keenly in mind. But I'm just saying that when my insides feel braided because I'm so worried about packing, a leaky roof, or an upcoming deadline, ten minutes curled up with my pink phone and the opinions of the unwashed masses is cozy with a capital *C*.

WORK

REMEMBER A COLLEAGUE at a restaurant where I worked as a waitress complaining in minute one of an eight-hour shift that she didn't want to be there. Perhaps it was a histrionic remark—we were in our twenties—but it struck me that it's what we did for at least eight hours every day. If she was unhappy all of that time, the math didn't work in her favor. Perhaps she would have been more content had she identified parts of herself that connected to joy in the space. For me, there was a lot that was cozy about Three of Cups in the East Village. It was fortifying when we were in the weeds, or slow with only one table of people eating. You could have a soda whenever you wanted—sounds small, but I kept a pint-sized glass of seltzer behind my workstation, and not for nothing, it was fun to come back and forth to and slurp on. I found the way the cooks in the kitchen communicated amusing and sexy. They sort of yelled at one another; it sounded like a family. There were one thousand candles in there. I loved my notepad for writing down orders, and kept it in the pocket of my apron as if it were a joey and I was a kangaroo. What the customers ordered interested me. Every table was a little adventure. The music we played was cool. If I tuned in and brought myself to the space, the hours flew. If my friend had zoned in on something even really small, like a fondness for the sneakers she chose to wear, she might have had a better time of it.

*   *   *

I AM NOT an office worker, so I reached out to friends.

Christine works in the mayor's office, so her civic response didn't surprise me: "People who put out big jars of candies or pretzels as a goodwill gesture toward others." Christine's whole life has been in public service; that she's buoyed by other people's awareness of the common good makes sense.

My friend Cristina runs her own office; therefore, she really has control of how she and the people who work with her spend their day.

> "I like having a sofa in my office where people can feel more relaxed, which hopefully generates creativity and honest discussion, but I like my desk to be sparse. I somehow believe that a clear desk lends to a clear mind. I always have tea in a cup and saucer—not a mug—because it makes me feel warm and cozy."

Even if you don't run the joint, you can always take control of your own space, so that you feel centered and reminded of your humanity.

Perhaps there are workplaces that have terribly strict rules where there is no allowance for personal effects—in these offices, one probably has to look even deeper inward. I would think that the work itself would have to provide you with a sense of well-being. For many, this is the case.

Nick is a writer, and he works in an office. His answer felt familiar to me, though I can't work with music playing.

"I like working in a hat. I just had a spoonful of peanut butter; that's cozy. I like to listen to background music. Right now I'm listening to a ten-hour mash-up of every 'Dark Star' the Dead performed in 1972. I do this often."

My brother works in an office in Washington, D.C.

"An office supply closet. Some well-funded offices have a cabinet where you can get a pencil or a yellow pad, but even just a communal pen cup has a coziness to it. Tools to do your job with are cozy."

My mother's office was formal but cozy. There was a little kitchen that had Pepperidge Farm Milano mint cookies in the cupboard. In the same room, there was a large copy machine. The *Star Wars*–like (it was the '70s) sound of someone Xeroxing was resoundingly cozy. For her, though, it was all about the elevator.

"The elevator going up to the office and back down to the street is cozy. Whether alone in the elevator or there with other people, it's a place to rev up or cool down, or just to daydream. It's fun to see who gets on and off—quite often people whom one has seen for years but doesn't know or speak to. *Oh, that person has a pretty new coat*, one observes, but no one says anything."

Peter's office is open for the most part, but they have three soundproof pods for making phone calls in a sturdy row along a wall. They are phone booths by any other name. Talking in those small, private spaces after being out in the open for many hours must be cozy, especially if he is talking to me.

QUILTING

❧

THE AIDS MEMORIAL Quilt was conceived of and started by the activist Cleve Jones. In 1985, Jones organized a march in San Francisco. He and his fellow protestors taped signs with the names of AIDS victims all over the San Francisco Federal Building. Jones thought it looked like a quilt and was inspired to start a movement where families and loved ones could make panels to honor the names of the dead. The panels were the dimensions of graves. Soon enough, panel by panel, it would amass into a Technicolor memorial quilt, big enough to cover the whole country—or at least the National Mall in Washington, D.C. At that time, because of fear, shame, and ignorance, the people who died of AIDS-related causes often didn't receive funerals or burials.

To me and my teenage friends growing up in New York City, there was nothing more terrifying than the AIDS epidemic. It was mysterious, dangerous, shrouded in secrecy, terrifically sad, and connected to the two things we all hoped for: intimacy and love. There isn't anything cozy about AIDS, but this audacious and powerful quilt that was growing and being displayed all over the world was comforting. People came together around that quilt. The squares that hundreds of husbands, mothers, sisters, lovers, and friends sewed, patchworked, appliquéd, collaged, and wove together are love letters and badges of courage. The quilt now weighs fifty-four tons and is the largest piece of folk art in America.

My friend Sarah is a quilter. When we were at RISD together, Sarah, with her short raven hair, was sort of like a punk-rock Betty Friedan. She spoke frankly, had a boyfriend with his own car (where I first heard Guns N' Roses), wore dark cherry-red lipstick that highlighted her big smile, and was the first graphic designer I ever met. I didn't know she could quilt. We might have been too young. Years later, there was evidence on her Instagram that quilts are a big part of her life. I went to Brooklyn to find out more.

"Quilts are sandwiches, basically." See, *sandwiches*— right off the bat we're deep in cozy talk. "What you are doing is sewing three layers together." She pulled at an unfinished quilt, showing me the batting and the supple cotton that was on either side of it. There was no narrative I knew of about that quilt, so the coziness was coming only from the touch of the soft fabrics, the organization of pattern, and the thread and needles. Sarah wanted to show me how the three pieces are sewn together because that's what makes a quilt a quilt, and why they have such a satisfying weight to them. She opened the door to her *sewing closet* and pulled out another quilt in progress. This closet, you have never—Betsy Ross herself would want to jump into it and roll around. On the back of the door must have been four hundred spools of thread on rows of pegs—a rainbow. Sarah's twelve-year-old twins, Kate and Abby, artists and sewers in their own right, sensed my awe of their closet and looked at me like, *Right?*

Sarah led me into her bedroom with the twins following behind like ducklings. In the corner of the sunlit room is a chair where the quilts live. They are folded and in a pile that reminded me of crepes.

"I started quilting when my father was dying," Sarah said, eyeing the heap as one looks for a favorite novel on a shelf, and pulled out a blanket. "He was in Massachusetts. I spent a lot of time in that house during that fall. One day, I picked up a book that was written in the eighteen hundreds about quilting, and read it. He was getting chemo, and I was sitting with him feeling . . . utzy . . . and needed something to do, so I started sewing. Over the next six months, I made a quilt and gave it to my father. He slept with it, and then he died with it."

She unfolded the soft, historic quilt over the one that she and her husband had slept under the night before, and smoothed her hand across it. "I never understood why people put quilts on walls. I've made something to provide warmth—why not use it for what it's made for?" After we admired it, Sarah pulled the quilt to her chest, held it there for a moment, and then started to fold it back up.

"After he died, I took a sabbatical to quilt." She flopped the final fold of her father's quilt so it looked like a square, put it on the top of the pile, then selected and pulled another quilt from the stack. (I gotta tell you, the ritual of folding and unfolding feels ceremonial.) "I sewed everything by hand at first—for a while, actually—before I started using a machine." She unfolds the quilt in her hand, lifts it with the help of her girls, and thumps it on her bed. I imagine, for Sarah's girls, the sound of quilt hitting quilt will always remind them of their mother.

"This was the next one I made. This was part of my grieving process." The quilt looks like the sea when there are clouds overhead. So many different colors of blues, bluey grays, patterns, textures, and underneath it all, invisible, but as obvious as the stitching, the tremendous story of father and daughter.

"The patches are all of my dad's suits and shirts." She looked at the quilt as if she were looking at him, and her girls looked at her, quietly knowing their mother was with her dad. She sighed, turned around, and went back to the pile cheerfully. "Each one of these has an important story— that's the thing with quilts." She looks for another example. "See—this is my pregnant quilt; this is the Sunday quilt." She pauses with her finger on top of the Sunday quilt. "Part of what is cozy about quilts is that you can take something you love, like a pair of blue jeans, and give it a new life. And here's the thing: in two hundred years, these might be all that's left of me." She yanks one of the corners and lifts it. "I sign each one." She smiles and tugs out another and is about to say something. "There are some . . ." But then she interrupts her reflections. "Oh, I wish everyone had a hobby that feels this cozy."

HOBBYING

❧

I T SEEMS TO me that when someone finds a hobby, it's because they have a natural affinity for it, an elevated level of skill, whether it's salsa dancing or Sudoku. It's yours. My hobby is cooking, and I'm pretty good at it for a number of reasons—my mother cooks; I love eating; I have children who need to eat; it's a nonverbal activity, so I could do it as a dyslexic; etc. It would stand to reason that a hobby grows out of the truth of who you are. *Or* perhaps your hobby was learned—you chose something unfamiliar; but you practiced whatever it is so well, it became second nature. Have you ever seen someone knitting in a lecture? They don't even need to look at the stitches and loops—*that's* second nature. When you can depend on an activity closely aligned with your essence and interest, I think it becomes cozy. A small skill that you don't necessarily earn a daily wage by doing. An active respite during the day.

I was an actress for twenty-five years. On movie and TV sets, there is a lot of downtime. If I was done memorizing lines, I tended to wander around the studio looking for a chat, but many actors could be seen tucked into corners, knees up, with a cup of something, a writing instrument, and *the crossword*. I would instantly assume that that actor, head down, hard at thinking, was smarter than your average bear, and I still do believe that it takes a certain kind of mind to enjoy a crossword puzzle. My upstairs neighbor Tracy has one of those minds.

"You have to make time for them. You think about them all day, turning them over and over—but you need the time to ruminate, relax, and clear your mind, no multitasking while crosswording! And I need a SHARPENED Blackwing pencil, with a neat eraser. If you're not a real crossword genius and expert (I am not), you have a real mess on your hands doing the Wednesday–Saturday puzzles in ink. I do them everywhere. I used to do the Mondays as a timed test from the moment the subway doors closed at the 103rd stop until they opened at Fiftieth Street. But at home, if it's a crossword day, I start at the breakfast table with the kids and we talk a little about the words, but I never finish them there. I will migrate to the bedroom, where my round table is and I can see the water. There I have my computer so I can check in with Rex Parker—who is the ninth-greatest crossword solver in the universe, does the puzzles early, and then blogs about them. The cozy part is there are some words and clues that appear again and again. Repetition, pattern, vocabulary—and memory."

Hobbies, as much as they are about personal skill, are also about connecting. Bonding with materials, your mind, a different language, nature. A friend's father is passionate about grass. He knows everything about heirloom grasses, varieties of grass, growth of grass. His daughter-in-law was describing his daily grass walks to me a few years ago and I can't get it out of my mind. A man in his seventies, slowly and peacefully staring out onto a marsh or field with the greatest concern and fascination with something most of us tread on every day without notice. Everybody cares about something different, so in a way, most things on earth are being paid attention to by somebody. That is hopeful.

Hobbies can span decades, even generations if you pass them on, like Irish step dancing. You take care of hobbies with maintenance, organization, and practice. Hobbies are unforced; you choose them, and they can be contagious. I tried to take up crocheting because my stepdaughter, Sage, does it. Sage is such a knitter, she and her pal started a club at their school. I love thinking about them sitting in a circle with other students and some teachers. They made a hobbying oasis for themselves right in the middle of a high school.

PART IV

JOURNEY

WE ARE A people on the move. Tourism is a multitrillion-dollar industry. There are migrations, refugees and displaced peoples, pilgrimages, and, long ago, nomadic migrations. Sometimes people travel from one side of the street to the other. Even Pa in *Little House on the Prairie* had to travel to Mankato to sell his lumber and get Ma and the girls a swath of calico to make a new Sunday dress. We move, and when there is movement, there is disruption. There is also coziness.

My husband, Peter, travels far and wide for work; he is the person I love most who travels the most. I asked him if there was anything cozy about his endless travel.

"Yeah, that I have it down pat," he said. "I know the terminals; there is a regularity to it all. Packing doesn't scare me anymore, because I know how to do it. I feel organized. It reminds me of suburbanites who commute to work: they all stand on the train platform in the exact place where they know the door is going to open." And then he paused. "You know what is actually cozy to me? If I'm traveling on a Sunday and there's a football game on. Even though I know I've left you and the kids, there's something, well, comforting about sitting in my seat with some work in front of me and watching a football game." His voice was soft and almost childlike, and it made me think that the reason why he feels like that is because he watched a lot of football growing up in his house on Long Island, with his twin brother and dad. He has found a piece of that sturdy upbringing thirty thousand feet in the air.

TRAVEL

🌿

"Men Wanted for Dangerous Expedition: Low Wages for Long
Hours of Arduous Labour under Brutal Conditions; Months of
Continual Darkness and Extreme Cold; Great Risk to Life and
Limb from Disease, Accidents and Other Hazards; Small Chance
of Fame in Case of Success."

—ERNEST SHACKLETON

I AM NOT A natural traveler. Some people find it the pinna-
cle of cozy—why? Adventure, seeking themselves in the
unknown, they moved around as kids, curiosity about other
lands and peoples. The food. In his memoir, Bruce Springsteen wrote about his life, lots of it spent on the road, "I felt
great elation at the wheel . . . it all felt like home . . ." But for
me it's a tough nut to crack.

Travel challenges familiarity and comfort, but hardly a
soul would make the case to stay at home. Looking at a map,
charting a course, is necessary to expand, walk in someone
else's shoes, grow one's point of view, gain perspective—
even the light looks different on one side of town from the
other, and it's good to see that. Noting the light anywhere
is a cozy thing to do because it's one of the easier ways we
can connect to nature. Have you ever heard of "God light"?

When sunbeams shine through low-lying stratus clouds? There has been many a troublesome time where I looked to the sky for God light.

Still and all, roving—even if your mind gets blown by pasta in Italy, a thatched roof, or a new language—is in its very nature disorienting and uprooting. To deal with being a stranger in a strange land, I would imagine that even the most *fernweh* nomads weave familiarity and routine into their escapades, small touchstones or habits to remind them of who they are.

Years ago, when I was pregnant, I read *Endurance: Shackleton's Incredible Voyage* by Alfred Lansing. The book recounts the expedition the master explorer Ernest Shackleton led from Norway to the Antarctic. I almost named the growing baby Shackleton, I was so impressed with his fortitude and ability to keep the crew moving forward and optimistic even when, in 1914, his schooner was mortally stuck in ice. Once the ship had sunk, he and his nineteen crew members survived for another two years until they reached civilization and rescue.

In an article about Shackleton for the *New York Times*, Nancy F. Koehn wrote, "He knew that in this environment, without traditional benchmarks and supports, his greatest enemies were high levels of anxiety and disengagement, as well as a slow-burning pessimism." Now, this is drastic, of course, but it makes me think about all movement and disruption of order. How do we keep the coziness? How did Shackleton do it? He was organized, kept journals, tried to stay warm, made lists, and relied on structure to get everyone from one day to the next. If we know that control and organization aid in coziness, it makes good sense to start any endeavor, especially one that takes you away from home, with a list. One more thing about lists: lists strike me as questions waiting to be addressed. What do you have control of? What do you want control of? Maybe nothing? When do you get cold, sick, exhausted? Can something on a list help you find comfort should any of these maladies occur?

I don't travel internationally very often, but for this book, I chose a few cities to explore coziness. Even though it sounds spoiled to say it, I wasn't enthusiastic to travel alone, leaving my husband and children and flying on airplanes. I wanted to stay at home. Leaving our well-honed routine felt chaotic, possibly irresponsible. I got in my head about it and had a few sleepless nights.

What I needed to do right away was impose order and make a list. I understand that many people who read this will cry out in agony, as the last thing some people think of as cozy is a list. But I go forth unafraid.

ISABEL'S TRAVEL QUESTIONS

What are you leaving? Where are you going?

Time change? Jet lag can compromise coziness, makes me feel the end is near—might be good to prepare for it mentally or with tricks like drinking a ton of water on the plane.

Clothes. Are you comfortable with your choices? You can change what you pack up until the very last minute.

Temperature. This is especially important if you are going somewhere cold. Do you have enough to keep you warm? Even warm climates can be chilly at night.

Take time to take care of what you're leaving. Watering the plants and making the bed will make the arrival home welcoming.

Important telephone numbers in case you lose your way?

Is it business travel, pleasure travel, tragedy travel, long-planned travel, unexpected travel? It's good to name your travel so you can adjust what you bring or even be aware of your mind-set.

Hotel bedrooms. What comes to mind? What do you want? Airbnb? Off the beaten path? On it?

Food and water. Is any of it going to make you sick? Do you care?

Prescriptions. Do you have what you need?

How old are you? It matters.

Itineraries. Do you have one? Do you stay in one place? Have a plan, or not have a plan?

Trains, planes, and automobiles. Which one do you feel the best about?

Passports and organization. Up to date?

Mistakes. What's the plan for failure?

Delays. Do you have something to do? See
   Hobbying.
Missed travel plans. Another bus always
   comes along, but when? Or do you care?
Packing. When will you begin?
Goals. What do you want out of your trip?
Guides, maps, articles. Information on where
   you are going? Or, we'll see when we get
   there?
Travel research. Or not? Some people want
   real discovery.
Food.
Who are you traveling with?
Language.

My friend Dewi is a consummate and frequent traveler. She lives in Europe and travels for work and to see her far-flung family. Seemed fitting to ask for her list.

Dewi's List

Sleep socks with rubber-dot soles for bathroom on
   plane
Travel with pashmina—chic and blanket
Comfy yet versatile pants
No jewelry, just makeup
Addicting series

Dark eye mask and silicone earplugs
Take one big carb. Bagel and banana—no plane food
    ever
One black trouser
One jeans
One bathing suit (never know)
One trainers and one versatile shoe loafer
Small amounts of all makeup, creams
Good PJs
Book
Be Euro, wear the same thing every day
Keep a little room in suitcase to buy souvenirs and gifts
Make sure your bag/knapsack/roller is not too heavy,
    make your journey a holiday from real strains
Go way in advance to airport, no stress
Put on earphones in lines, don't wear stuff you have to
    take off in security

The person whom I most associate with travel is my childhood friend Bess. Somewhere along the way during our forty-year friendship, we started calling each other Rudy. Rudy is always on the go.

Rudy on Travel

"I think my main thing would be to bring the cozy with you. Bring a teeny pillow and set it right away on the bed. Always have a nice shawl and spread it over the bed as needed (sometimes the bedcovers are depressing). Always unpack right away and place your homey, cozy objects around the room. And if there is a bath, immediately take one and soak in the place. Always find cozy neighborhood spots for coffee and general supplies. Don't leave your kit with a *k* packed either. Move into the space as much as possible, like it's a nest. In China, at the Monkey King Hotel, I always remember my hotel room that I lived in for six weeks. I adored the view (this is very important—you must find something to cherish in your view even if it's not textbook pretty). I had a BEAUTIFUL weeping willow outside my window in China and some sort of whitewashed nothing wall beside a little kind of creek—but it looked so Chinese I practically died of happiness.

Also, if there are routines at home that you enjoy, like jogging, definitely keep them up abroad. No reason to abandon the habits that bring you joy and make you feel like yourself simply because you're in a different city! I can remember runs in France in champagne country at eighteen, France in vineyards all those Bordeaux years, millions of Italian runs. It also makes you truly know a place to navigate it like that. So maybe if people don't jog, they should be sure to go on long walks to know their territory.

I remember arriving in China alone and pretty scared. I walked down the street to a market and ate a peach. It was so familiar that it made me calm down a bit. A peach is a peach the world over!"

DENMARK

ITH ITS CITIZENS clad in layers, bicycle culture, and "window weather," Denmark (and all of Scandinavia, really) is famously cozy. Each country has its own word describing a warm, connected feeling; *koselig* in Norway, *mysig* in Sweden, and *hygge* in Denmark. I chose to go to Denmark, but *hygge* is not why I went to Denmark—*Hamlet* is.

I read Shakespeare's dark, psychological tragedy at age fifteen and swore I would one day visit Elsinore. I identified with Ophelia, Hamlet's girlfriend. The inky Danish prince cloaked in anxiety felt like every teenage lad I ever fell for—most of whom dumped me. Somewhere very real in my adolescent catastrophe of a brain, I *got it* when Hamlet damned Ophelia to a nunnery and then when she dramatically threw herself into an icy brook. I totally got *Romeo and Juliet* too—those first bouts with love are category five, and all outcomes seemed plausible to me as a young romantic person. When something, even a gloomy tragedy, hits home, feels authentic, strikes a chord, it's cozy. We're complicated creatures who think crazy thoughts and feel emotion so deeply it brings us to our knees. We need to connect with art or stories to feel less alone in that humanity—it's soothing to know someone else felt it too. I had a boyfriend who carried around a tattered copy of *The Brothers Karamazov* in his saxophone case like a philosophical baby blanket. You wouldn't think that the long-haired rocker would be bound to the ethical debates of God, but he was. I mean, heck, I find Mozart's requiem cozy, and it's about death! Even on an excursion to find cozy in other lands, going to Elsinore, home of the dark prince, presented as far cozier than anything *hygge* I'd heard about.

Anyway, off to Denmark I went.

"The first condition to understanding a foreign country is to smell it," Rudyard Kipling wrote. When I reached the shores of Denmark, every sense in my body was turned on so I could be open and available to *hygge*. I expected just by my touching Danish soil, *hygge* would wrap its arms around me. Within hours, I was let down. With Kipling's words in my mind, I inhaled deeply standing on the taxi line, hoping to smell fog. Having been raised partially in Maine, fog conjures romance, seafaring life, and sweatshirts, and for some reason (probably because of *Hamlet*) I expected fog. But it was a sunny day. Onward. In the back seat of the taxi, I eagerly looked out the window and did see *hygge* things, red rooftops, Danes wrapped in woolen scarves and blue jeans holding paper cups of coffee, bikes, bread shops. But here's the tricky part: even when I cupped my hands around a Danish ceramic mug brimming with milky foam and hot coffee, or noticed that there were blue wool blankets neatly folded over all of the chairs in outdoor cafés, heard a bell ring as I exited a bakery and ripped into a still-warm flaky croissant—to my surprise and disappointment, I didn't feel cozy, or connected to any of it.

Layered sweaters alone do not make one cozy. What I was uncovering in real time in the land of the north was that if I wanted coziness, even if it felt unfair and exhausting after traveling all that way expecting that it would magically be available to me, I had to work at it. I wanted *so much* to feel really good inside just by being in the country where *hygge* was born. I wanted the glow of the candles to instantly translate to a glow inside of me, but it didn't happen. In fact, at first, I felt alienated and alone, even on a cobblestone street. What did I have to do to get some of that *hygge*?

TO MAKE MATTERS worse (for the time being), I hadn't gotten an international phone plan. Unless I wanted to go broke because of astronomical roaming charges, the phone would stay in my pocket and turned off. Even though my knee-jerk reaction was to call home, being freed of what everyone else in my life was doing thousands of miles away, I was forced to slow down and sop up my surroundings. What soon became clear was that a defining characteristic of *hygge* was simply being present.

There are a lot of outdoor cafés in Copenhagen, and every table was crammed with people having a drink and chatting. What struck me most, probably because I didn't have mine, was the lack of phones. At one particularly hopping café, I counted *only one person* on a phone, and that guy was standing up as if he had just excused himself to check a text. I'm sure Apple could prove me wrong—the Danes are probably just as addicted as we are—but it didn't feel that way. People looked to be tête-à-tête no matter where I went. The chatting became my focus, and I began to feel cozy, even though I didn't speak the language. I asked a bartender about the crush of conversation I was noticing: to Thea, the louder the café or bar, the more *hygge*. "This place is *hygge* because it's so loud with chatter—it's relaxed, you can talk about all sorts of things you want to talk about—*good things*, things you don't want to talk about on a quiet bus."

There were buses in Copenhagen, but as you might expect, bicycles ruled the transportation scene. Like fish, the people of Copenhagen darted and zoomed around on bikes in great schools. Most bikes had large buckets affixed to their fronts. Piled in them were fresh-faced girlfriends swathed in multiple woolen scarves, dogs, older people. And nobody was riding like pumpkins in carts; most were in conversation with the person peddling, or with their companion in the bucket. Togetherness seemed to be the order of the day. Coziness emerged like a ship from the fog.

> "Handheld food rights our wrongs,
> turning a bad world briefly good."
> —NIGEL SLATER

Before my journey, I bought Magnus Nilsson's *The Nordic Cookbook*, a four-hundred-pounder of Scandinavian food, history, and culture. Nilsson is a Nordic chef who, with his scruffy beard, long hair, and twinkly eyes, looks like a Viking. I was taken with his Norse hunter-gatherer ways while watching a food series on TV. Nilsson ice fishes, kneels in piney woods to pick wild sorrel, and risks his life traversing the steep cliffs of Stóra Dímun to gather fulmar eggs. He owns a restaurant called Fäviken way in the north of Sweden that celebrates the history, culture, and geography of the lands close to him. In particular, he embraces the food Scandinavians grew up with and already have in their larders. National pride, seeing and loving what's already there—it's all fucking cozy because HE finds it cozy, and you can tell on the page.

My focus in Nilsson's all-encompassing bible became the time-honored Nordic sandwich *smørrebrød*. He writes, "Its origins can be traced back for more than a millennium and it exists in hundreds of variants. An open cheese sandwich speaks of the most fundamental aspects that make up a food culture in the Nordic region, but also demonstrates that a 'taste chord' can live a very long time if it's important to people and provides meaning." The idea of a "taste chord" struck me as fundamentally cozy—a harmony of personal taste, culture, identity, and temperature.

And as Nilsson had promised, there were sandwiches everywhere in Copenhagen. They were so omnipresent, I asked the concierge in my tiny hotel for help in finding an especially Danish one. He pointed me in the direction of a "place at the bottom of a little stairs" for *smørrebrød*—and where *hygge* would be thick. Handwritten map in gloved hand, I went walking along the cobblestones, noting every little round ancient window with glass bulging in the frames, where most of the time there was a candle glowing.

Nestled at the bottom of the "little stairs" was the Scandi

restaurant that turned out to be the epicenter of my *hygge* journey. It was *Architectural Digest*'s version of a Beatrix Potter rabbit warren. Whitewashed walls and exposed dark wooden beams glowed in candlelight. There was a sheepskin over the back of each midcentury caned chair, and the entire menu was *smørrebrød*. The waiter, Jeppe, suggested ordering two or three. Soon plates piled with smoked salmon, chicken, and buttermilk-whipped-butter arrived, and as if he were presenting the keys to the city, Jeppe also placed a grey woolen envelope beside my plate.

"Pocket bread," he said oh so proudly. I opened and pulled out a thick slice of warm dark rye. "You serve all your bread in this?" I asked, feeling the earthiness of the rye. It felt like something you would find in the forest. "Oh yes! There is a woman up the street who made eighty of these pockets for us. It's called *kuvertbrød* [a play on the French word for "place setting"]—a piece of bread cut squarely so it can fit in a pocket." Clearly, any young man who serves lunch like a child showing you an art project was someone I had to engage in the conversation of *hygge*.

"*Hygge*—hold on, let me go in the kitchen and ask the others." He dashed away. Balancing the slice in one hand, I began piling forkfuls of creamy celeriac, poached chicken, and gherkins onto the Danish *rugbrød*. My other *smørrebrød* was flannel-like ribbons of roast beef topped with fried onions and a silken egg whose marigold-orange yolk melted down and around every corner. The heaping and soaking-up opportunities had room for variation or repetition; up to you.

After consulting his peers, Jeppe returned to thoughtfully present his views on *hygge* in English, but to hear it with the Danish accent—whoosh. "The thing about *hygge* is—you can do it with your grandma, or your girlfriend, or alone. It's a wonderful feeling inside." He stood there with his hand on his chest and became just a little bit verklempt. "Yah, see"—he took a breath and collected himself—"that's the thing about my job! I always think it's *hygge!*"

His emotion hit me in my core, for I too was a waiter, and felt the same way Jeppe did about it. *God, I LOVED being a waiter.* Coziest job I ever had. I loved serving hungry people. The East Village restaurant where I worked was filled with candles and a wood-burning oven. We didn't have pocket bread, but there was a bottle of olive oil on every table so you could have as much as you liked. Lenny, my boss and one of the owners of the place, set the tone. In his stoic rock-and-roll way, Lenny just wanted people to be happy. Lenny was from Atlanta and knew the Black Crowes. He looked like he could have been a member of the Clash: white T-shirts rolled up at the sleeves, blue jeans, and spiffy shoes. He had tattoos all over his arms.

Lenny once told me that he found pitting olives cozy—yes, he actually said "cozy." It's funny to think about now since in *no way* did he vibe Jamie Oliver (though he did ripen tomatoes on our windowsills). When he mumbled the thing about the olives, he was at the pizza station in front of the fire. Elton John's *Tumbleweed Connection* (if you don't know that album, get it right now) was playing. As he pressed Kalamata olive after Kalamata olive against a cutting board, extracting the pit without hurting the fruit, he pointed out that the task was methodical. He said it helped him collect his thoughts before dinner service. The more he pitted, the more he knew we would be prepared for the night. It was comforting, he said. Lenny died while he was still in his twenties of a heroin overdose. And he's with me every time I cook.

ENGLAND

❧

THE MOTHERLAND OF cozy is England. Of course, this isn't true for everyone, but even though my Anglophilia is so white-bread and old-fashioned, I can't help it—I've felt a seismic pull since I was a child hiding under the piano secretly watching the BBC's *Upstairs, Downstairs* when my parents thought I was asleep. It was written in the sand that I make a cozy pilgrimage there because, well . . . *Chariots of Fire*; lapsang souchong and trucker teas; roses; butchers; English accents; Jamie Oliver and Hugh Grant; curries; beans and toast; Victoria sandwich cake; fried shrimp scampi; pasties and Cadbury English Flake; dog culture; Hogwarts; parks; manners; the Beatles, bagpipes, and the Rolling Stones; *Wolf Hall* and *Downton Abbey*; row houses; *The Great British Baking Show* and *HELLO!* magazine; the Tube; all monarchs going back to the 800s; Floris bath oils; rain; Jane Austen, Emily Brontë, Merchant Ivory, Virginia Woolf; tartans; thistles; Nigel Slater; sheep; rolling hills; Dickens. I get it that a lot of this is fattening food, murderous monarchs, and heartbreak, but it's in my blood.

The bigger picture here, of course, is *not* that England is the be-all-end-all of cozy, but rather that if you think about who you are, gather your personal experience, and meditate on what you feel connected to, you can journey literally or figuratively to a place that brings you great comfort. I have a jug of thistles sitting right in front of me in New York City because I know every time I look at them, I feel solid—a puzzle piece has settled in. The prickly, spiky bloom happens to be the floral emblem of Scotland.

* * *

THE FIRST DAY in England, I met up with long-time pal Nina at the train station and off we went on the Tube to the Tower of London.

Nina had been studying gardening at the English Gardening School, so we talked a lot about that on the way there, and as I wasn't going to visit a garden, I pulled out my notepad.

"I think gardening in England is cozier than anywhere else. Maybe also cozy in other places, but not as cozy—and roses are the coziest of all. Brits have a really tender and important relationship with their roses."

Nina went on as I took notes.

"Maybe picking flowers and arranging them is quite cozy. [Agreed—see the flower chapter.] I suppose planting bulbs is really the coziest, as you're making little homes for them, away from harm and danger—it's very much about finding them a private, nourishing place to wait out the season and then really rooting for them to pop up and out and visit."

Soon we were at the Tower of London. Succumbing is a huge part of coziness—giving in, fully committing. In a museum, that could mean getting the map, investing in the audio guide, or perhaps simply breathing. Your imagination can do its job more effectively when you breathe.

Just as she'd said she would, Nina gave in to all things 1500s England. We donned our earphones, linked arms, and ventured into the past. A very important part of being cozy is letting yourself get swept away by the narrative as if you were a child. The problem with cynicism or resistance in a place like a museum is that it robs you of asking the important question, *What if? What if* you were a courtier in Henry VIII's court? *What if* you got to wear the crowns and silk robes with embroidered thistles? *What if* you were Anne Boleyn, locked away in the dark, cold, wet tower?

LIST OF COZY THINGS
ABOUT THE TOWER OF LONDON

- Audio guide (true of all historical sites)
- Following a map
- The Thames River—natural landmark
- Ancient stones—imagining how many centuries of people have trod on them
- Waiting in line with people from other nations—2.5 million people a year visit
- Languages
- Learning (what the kings' beds were made of, how many layers—could see them all)
- School trips led by a woman dressed as a nun from the 1500s (reminded me of *Madeline*)
- Embroidered thistles on coronation robes—powerful symbols—scepters, orbs, swords, crowns
- Acknowledging with a friend silently when you simultaneously hear an interesting fact on the guided tour
- Thinking about where to go for lunch
- Pausing the audio guide now and again to sit on a bench and take in the history, and discuss with friend
- Imagine what it would feel like if you lived at that time
- Souvenir shops (got Christmas ornaments of King Henry VIII and Ann Boleyn)

PUBS WITH MARK

"Our troubles are all the same . . ."

—*Cheers* THEME SONG

ARS: JEWEL-BOX HOTEL bars, dives, honky-tonks, pubs—
some sleek or luxurious, some dingy, many with great
names, all cozy. Because of the variety of establishments,
straightaway I have to ask if the element that makes them
united in coziness is the booze. I think we are obliged to
name it and say yes. I get that it's the place where everyone knows your name, and community is one of the four
pillars of cozy, but possibly, it's the drink. I have many
friends who have wreaked havoc on themselves and others
in the four walls of a bar. It seems irresponsible to include a
chapter that could be triggering. And I'm thinking of that
haunting folk song from the 1800s, "Come Home, Father,"
about the little girl who is begging her dad to come home
from the bar because she and her mother are nursing her
sick and dying brother—who dies while the father drinks
away the doomed night. So it's not without hesitation that
I want to plow ahead and say, *BARS ARE COZY!* Some of
my most unseemly behavior was acted out in bars. I'm not

an alcoholic, but I will divulge I had my hand in sloppiness, emotional dysregulation, and bad choices made in some dive or another in New York City, usually on the Lower East Side.

That said, bars *are* undeniably cozy. On some mornings, I'll be walking down a street, scrubbed and ready for a day, and I'll pass by a bar. It will be shut and quiet, but the resilient fragrance of stale beer loiters outside its door. The smell of wet, oaty brew from the previous night sparks a cozy feeling of belonging. The smell is a connection to a warm past of dancing, laughing, kissing, gossiping, being twenty-one, free, in a tribe, protected by a meaty bouncer or a devoted pack of sweaty friends, smoking, peeling labels off Budweisers, doing shots with the band, a jukebox. But even now, when I sidle up to the most civilized of bars to order ONE solidly fortysomething cocktail, I get a cozy feeling in me. It's all about the sturdy mahogany to lean on, the hum and chatter, the bartender concentrating on mixing, the stool, the icy rocks glass, the other souls, and this very distinct awareness that I'm in the middle of a collective story. Maybe it's *civilization*.

I didn't have to travel to England to visit a pub, as there are two similar establishments (a college bar and a jazz club) within spitting distance of my apartment, but one imagines the very first pub was born on England's mountains green. You can research and discover that *tabernae* are as old as the Roman empire, but even if you read every last book on the topic, pubs from time immemorial are simply places where a community gathers to eat and drink. The Fox and the Sword, The King's Fiddle, The Raven's Claw—names of pubs and bars are epic, even if the establishment is just called "bar."

In London, my friend Mark and his brother Dom very kindly took me out on a pub crawl for this book. The surprisingly cozy part wasn't the barkeeps out of central casting, or the scampi and peas on the hand-sized menu, or even the iconic pint glasses brimming with creamy Guinness—it was these brothers. As we slid into a wooden booth that looked like it had been there since Queen Victoria's reign, and they, in a rather Hugh Grantian way, inquired what I would like to drink so one of them could go up and get it for me (classic English manners—I don't care if it's the accents, they all roundly seem to have been raised by Mary Poppins), I could sense their brotherhood. I don't know if that particular pub was where they had found shelter from the dank English rain as young lads. Did they holler about a football game or cavort with university pals there? Was this the place they discussed marriage proposals, or worried about their parents? I felt it was intrusive to ask such personal questions, but it sure felt like we were on tried-and-true stomping grounds. The brothers were *comfortable* in there, as if it was something in their chemical makeup. They knew the language, rhythms, and traditions intrinsically.

Because it was their assignment of the evening, they dutifully regaled me with heritage and history of pubs in England, architectural characteristics of low ceilings and beams, assuring menus of scotch eggs and stout pies, ales and shandies (for the ladies, wink). But I barely listened because even though the assessments of what made pubs cozy to them were true and worth taking note of, it was the two of them in the setting that hit the chord. They could have been any brothers in any country of any race or creed. The point was they were together in their corner of the world. It was the connection that was cozy, the two of them with their pints and little bags of crisps.

WALKS

"The true charm of pedestrianism does not lie in the walking, or in the scenery, but in the talking. The walking is good to time the movement of the tongue by, and to keep the blood and the brain stirred up and active; the scenery and the woodsy smells are good to bear in upon a man an unconscious and unobtrusive charm and solace to eye and soul and sense; but the supreme pleasure comes from the talk."

—MARK TWAIN

WALKING STICKS, WALKING meetings, walking shoes, getting ready for a walk, walking tours, linking arms and walking, walking paths, walking for your heart and bones, walking in the city, walking in the woods, walking with a kid. Even the word "stroll" is cozy. Something about rolling along, forward-looking, getting somewhere new or checking in with the familiar. There is a class in my kids' middle school called Walking with Walkup. For forty minutes, rain or shine, the students march around the neighborhood led by Mr. Walkup. The good this does for everyone—including the teachers who get the kids for the following class—could and should probably be measured, but since there is no way to do that, I picked up the phone and asked Ms. Berkery, who is the eyes, ears, and nose of the school. She said simply, "It gives the kids a sense of belonging."

This is what I'm talking about! This is why walking to the mailbox is a cozy thing to do. In this class, the middle schoolers are connecting with their local environment during the day, which provides perspective—they are exposed to the world: businesspeople, homeless people, mail carriers, shopkeepers, buses, the sidewalk itself. They bring all of that intelligence back with them into their history or math classes. And, of course, they are strolling with friends, and walking with a friend is the coziest of all—add a dog, off the charts.

If I said I traveled across an ocean to go on a walk with my childhood friend Vanessa, who lives deep in the English countryside, that would be a true statement. I only had one day in her brick house in the village, and after the children had gone to school, husband to work, breakfast dishes washed, coffee sipped at kitchen table, beds made, we got on wellies—oh yes we did—leashed Hazel, who is a lurcher (looks like a wiry greyhound, very English), and set off to the moors. Now, technically, they are miles of gargantuan rolling working fields, but looking back, I can't help but think of them as the windswept downs in *Wuthering Heights*.

I was about to go into a long description of trudging over hill and dale with my beloved friend. Talking is productive and satisfying when one walks. I think it's the blood flow to the brain. In fact, "walking meetings" are trendy for that very reason. Get out, take in fresh air, get the heart moving. And as I had hoped back in New York, Ness and I did walk and saw great big thistles, cows with curly thick heads grazing, and met a few villagers as we went. Hazel ran like

the wind ahead of us, always circling around to check in before she did it again. Dogs, nature, community—cozy! But
something about this makes me sad. What if you didn't have
a friend to walk with? There have been times in my life when
I have felt friendless. I think many people sometimes feel
there isn't a friend in the world whom they could take a walk
with. This is when cozy is the most important, and when it's
the hardest to see. I'm going to stand by walking. I believe
that even in a friendless moment, a walk will make you feel
better. It goes back to what Ms. Berkery said: "It gives the
kids a sense of belonging." When you walk, you are retold
that you belong to the world and that the world is lucky to
have you. A step is cozy.

ALONE TIME

❧

I DIDN'T THINK I would feel lost and alone in London—but I most certainly did. A little jet-lagged, a little sick, gone one too many days from my kids, I felt rudderless. The unfamiliar streets seemed daunting, and I wanted to give up on the whole project. *Who cares if London is cozy or not?* I thought. Really! Who cares? There were wars being fought, refugees trying to find a home, Brexit had just been voted on. In our country, the results of an embittered and astounding election had left everyone reeling. Who the bloody hell cared about small things anymore? But in every time of personal upheaval and reckoning, the smallest parts of life have been the only things powerful enough to pull me through.

So, standing on an ordinary-enough-looking street, what I asked myself was, *How can I attach to something? How can I bring something true about who I am and hook it into this city?* I thought that if I was able to ground myself if only for a minute, I would then be able open the aperture, let in my surroundings, and keep going with the order of the day. Was there a tree I liked? A telephone booth? Peering in the windows, I felt like an anxious teenager unable to find a seat in the cafeteria. What could I see? Turned out it was a name:

PAUL. I've always liked that name, and there it was in bold letters over the bread counter of a coffee shop. Seeing it, I felt a tug of familiarity, a sense of calm, a sense that all would be okay once I was seated inside. It was a spark of a feeling, but enough of one that I fanned the flame and opened the door.

Inside, people were chatting, working, reading the paper in a similar way to what I might find in my neighborhood at home. On the wall there was a sign that read, *Our family has been making bread with a passion since 1889*. There were no corners left, so I chose a place to sit near the wall where it would be easy to observe while I drank frothy misto and ate a croissant. Next to me, three Israeli women were sipping coffee and tucking into gossipy, giggly chat. They could have been a group of moms I knew taking a break after school drop-off. I noticed how much I loved my sturdy watch. To my right, there was some sort of tutoring lesson. The teacher and student were battling particularly flakey pastries that were making a mess of their math work. It was run-of-the-mill, recognizable, and as though it were a chemical change, I could feel my attitude adjusting and arranging itself in a positive way.

When I left *PAUL* fortified and centered, the rest of my wandering seemed manageable. A book shop straight out of a Mike Nichols rom-com appeared around a corner, and I bought the paperback of the novel *All the Light We Cannot See*. A few blocks down was a butcher who sold real English hand pies—treasures displayed through an old-fashioned window. I chose one filled with chicken and peas for lunch, which, if I could swing it, I would eat in a park while I read my new book. It was a little nippy, but I was prepared with a large scarf in my backpack to wrap around me. The book and the scarf were stepping-stones, and by having them, my willingness to explore and absorb the city was full-on—I was even okay with getting lost, which I promptly did—and that's how I found the park. "All who wander are not lost" is a favorite J. R. R. Tolkien quote in our household. Wandering for some is the coziest of all because there is freedom, bravery, creativity, and spirit in *not* knowing what lies ahead—it goes back to Shackleton, and Bruce Springsteen!

You don't have to be in a foreign country to feel far away. When my first husband told me he was leaving, I felt lost in my own kitchen. When my father had a stroke, I felt lost in my own driveway. When my dog died at the vet when I wasn't with her, I felt lost in my own bed. The questions are: What will bring you back? What will help you find your way? How can you survive the disorientation? I think besides radical, bold moves often required to walk another mile, sometimes a good place to start is by holding your reading glasses in your palm, wrapping a scarf around your neck, or listening for birdsong in a tree above.

PART V

WHEN IT
FEELS
HARD

"Everybody hurts, sometimes."

—R.E.M.

"THAT MUST FEEL hard" is something my mother said to all us kids whenever life hurt. And it can hurt so often. The phrase is just an acknowledgment—it never changed what was difficult, but it did make it feel better. So much of cozy you can touch with your hands—a book, bathwater, a mug—but a lot of cozy responds to the ether, the mystic, the ritual and spiritual.

This section is about bringing your A-game to cozy. These circumstances are when you'll have to put to work your cozy tools, and it may not come easily. These are the times when one thinks there is no hope or place for something like a breakfast tray—but in fact, the breakfast tray might be the very thing that anchors you and pulls you through.

HOSPITAL

I F YOU ARE in a hospital, there is coziness to be identified. Hospitals are challenging—and they are also places where you get help. This reminds me of the famous piece of advice Mr. Rogers gave when soothing children during national crises where they might see upsetting pictures in the newspapers. "Look for the helpers," he urged. Even in horrifying depictions of fires or shootings, there is almost always a first responder in the frame coming to someone's rescue.

If you find yourself in a hospital, look for the helpers— there are hundreds of them. Police and guards know who is coming through the doors, and why. Intake, the keepers of information. Nurses and PAs, medical technicians, all variety of specialists, janitors, the people who work in the cafeterias and flower shops. Sure, it's a business, and these people are employed—but don't let that make you cynical; they have chosen a life of caretaking. Hospitals are teeming with volunteers, therapy dogs, people who read aloud to those who can't. One can derive strength from what these souls are doing, even by just watching them. Can you listen for an accent you might connect with? Does someone look like they would be able to answer your questions? Most people who work in hospitals have name tags—this is useful. It can make you feel closer and more protected just to know someone's name. Notice how good people are at their jobs. Observing a nurse cutting a bandage or a doctor listening to a cough is pretty amazing. These are healers. Does it make you feel better knowing there are medical procedures practiced all the time? Millions of routines that have been carefully considered and memorized. Very much like jury duty, one might feel cozy knowing how much effort the people who work at hospitals put into protocol.

You can go even more granular. Twelve years ago during a stay at Brigham and Women's Hospital in Boston, I noticed that the ice cubes dispensed from the machine on my floor were shaped like elongated pencil erasers, and they were softer than your average cube. If I coated them in one or two pushes from the Pepsi machine, the spongy ice would absorb the cola just enough to taste good, while keeping a firm texture that was rewarding to bite into. The paper cups provided were very big and fit into the crook of my elbow and hip. The weight and temperature soothed my tender body. Throughout the day I would plan and look forward to my trips to the soda machine to make the healing concoction. Who would I see at the nurse's station? What time would the big, round hallway clock say? Would I run into the orderly who winked at me the day before? Was there a new posting on the bulletin board? All of those internal monologues were part of my quest for coziness during that hospital time. I once saw on Twitter there is a hospital cafeteria in Houston that has a cobbler bar. A COBBLER BAR. Come on, someone who understands cozy is working there for sure.

Pepsi ice cubes and peach cobbler do not change the reason you are in the hospital, but they or something like them, like the blanket-warming ovens, might make the experience more breathable—even, in moments, enjoyable.

MAMMOGRAMS

L ET'S BE VERY clear: getting a mammogram is not only physically unpleasant, painful sometimes, but it's upsetting to the core. Even though you are facing the truth, and facing the truth is ultimately the best thing to do, everyone in the room is tender, everyone is vulnerable, and everyone is handling some degree of uncertainty. There is a hushed worry that you soak in the moment the elevator doors open on the radiology floor. You also feel cold. In order to keep the imaging machines working properly, it must be a certain temperature—and it's not a warm one.

At my last mammogram, sitting in a robe trying not to invade anyone's privacy with my eyes, I noticed the cover of a book, framed, leaning on the windowsill. It was a coloring book called *Lost Oceans*. Around the title of the book swirled drawings of bubbling seaweed, octopi, coral, currents, angelfish. In print below, it said, *PAGES AVAILABLE FOR YOUR USE, PLEASE FEEL FREE TO ASK THE FRONT DESK FOR A CLIPBOARD.* As I took this surprising gesture in, I thought that I would *love* to do some restorative, distracting coloring at that moment. As a person who wants to draw all the time, the book got my attention. As if I were looking to identify the person who had the good coloring-book idea, I noted what the staff was doing. Every few moments, someone would come to offer a soft, well-worn, clean blanket to put over knees. Coffee, tea, and hot water were set up in the back of the waiting room. I was asked twice if I was cold, and I noted there were small space heaters distributed and nestled near the chairs. The heaters could easily be turned on without a lot of fuss.

Nobody in the entire hospital can take away how unnerving, sad, or mysterious it is to have a mammogram, but someone was certainly making an effort to help people get through it.

That waiting room modeled some behavior for me, and reinforced the idea that you have a hand in your experiences. Sometimes we think we don't, that we will just career through the (endless) less-than-pleasant things like mammograms. However, there are two things at play here: mammograms are terrible, *and* if we take some control, we can have a better time of it. Can you build serenity before you even leave the house? Do you think your facility will have tea and coffee? If not, is there a place nearby where you can stop first and bring it with you ? Or even a Martinelli's apple juice? Do you have a gripping magazine article that will keep your attention or possibly provide perspective? A pack of spicy gum? Do you have the right clothes on? What are those clothes? Tidy? Soft? Easy to remove and put back on? Are you armed for the fear or uncertainty with things that make *you* feel good? I suppose a companion could be comforting, but most of the time I go for a mammogram, I go alone.

I remember waiting in the pediatrician's office with the

boys when they were very small, two and four. I knew it was just a routine checkup, but they had no real idea of why they were in there. We moved around a lot when the boys were small, and didn't have a familiar pediatrician to ease any ambivalent feelings they may have had about being in a doctor's office. I could see the anxiety in their delicate shoulders under the paper robes. My instinct was to distract by describing the tools and machines. If you have knowledge about your surroundings, it can feel less intimidating. But there was only so much I knew (*This is what they look in your ears with!*) and the distraction wasn't hugely satisfying. What I settled on was counting from one to one hundred. We would lean against the wall and count. If the doctor wasn't there by one hundred, we'd start again. I didn't know at the time if this methodical counting had any effect until recently, when I was sitting in a doctor's office with Thomas, who is now fourteen and six foot four. The doctor was delayed, and we were sitting in silence. I was about to get out my phone and anxiously scroll, and then I heard my kid's voice: "One, two, three."

NURSE

THE FIRST THREE doctors I asked about hospitals and coziness—without missing a beat—instantly said, "You need to talk to the nurses," so my mission was to go find a nurse. Enter Ann Finck. Ann has spent forty-five of her seventy-two years in the critical care neurointensive unit at NewYork–Presbyterian Hospital, mostly at "bedside." She worked with a doctor friend of mine. Ann was in charge of tending to very sick patients who couldn't get out of bed. Most of them were recovering from strokes, craniotomies, aneurysms, and severe traumas. "For whatever reason," Ann said, holding a cup of coffee, "bedside didn't tire me. I loved it—it was my sweet spot. Hospitals *are* cozy, and ICUs are where coziness is needed."

"Well," she said, and gathered her thoughts. "There are thousands of ways to make someone cozy. There are thousands of patients, and what makes one person cozy won't necessarily make another person cozy. Coziness is something you have to figure out patient to patient and family to family—they are both critically ill. Understanding is cozy because people want to know how they are being taken care of. Makes them feel better."

She had a bite of spinach omelet and continued. "There are universal 'hows.' One question is, 'How does a person feel in the bed, and how does a person look in the bed?' In my rooms—and people used to say that my rooms were 'Annasized'—there was no clutter, they were neat, clean, comfortable, and restful. There are many, many IVs. I made sure each one was lined up and labeled. It made *me* feel calm and organized. It was very important to me that the patient's face and hands were clean, that their hair was combed and the bed was tidy. I think it was important for the families, who are so worried."

Ann's confidence and intelligent, calm demeanor made me feel cozy sitting next to her, like a dream grandmother, but one who could stabilize my heart.

"Information is important. In the ICU, the patient is surrounded by machinery—it's scary and upsetting. Explaining to the families what you are doing and what the machines are is an important comfort measure."

While thinking about what was cozy, she smiled, like she had remembered a specific patient in her care.

"I used to do something called Breezes. You see, in the ICU, you have to turn the patient every two hours so they don't get bedsores. It's very hard to make someone comfortable, and it's hard to tell if they are comfortable because they are so sick. Some of them can't talk, some are unconscious . . . but you want them to feel good, so you ask, *Does that make you feel better?* And sometimes you have to guess based on what makes you yourself feel better. So, I always thought it would be nice, before the bed was tucked in, to flutter the sheet over the patient, to cool them off, or just because the breeze could send a message that someone cared."

BLOOD

❧

LOCATING COZINESS IN the hospital, the wilderness, or a war zone is one thing, but most of us are not called to do that. The more likely experience is that something troubling occurs in and around your home, and these smaller troubles happen with great frequency.

Everything's fine. This is something Dad always says whenever he has any information to impart so there is no sudden worry, and so the person hearing the news doesn't think they have to jump into any kind of action—basically, nothing is on fire. (Dad once called me and said, "Everything's fine, but Grandpa died.")

Dad had a stroke several years ago. All was okay and he recovered by himself, with very few physical effects. However, the medicine he was prescribed and took continually made his blood very thin. Years after the stroke, I was spending the summer in my parents' house writing this book. The children were away on summertime adventures; my husband, Peter, was working down in the city; and my days were filled by writing, cooking, and walking the dogs. I got a routine, a schedule, a groove, and life was grand. Then one day, Dad came into my working room with blood spilling quickly and profusely from his nose. Because of the blood thinner, this was not a good situation. I drove him to the health center, my mother met us, and she and the professionals took over. They checked him into a hospital.

Back at the house, and for the next few days, life not only felt uncertain, but it was a bummer—sorry to use that term; it sounds intolerant and surfer-like, but sometimes "bummer" is just the best word.

The sink my father had been standing over was filled and splattered with his bright red blood, and it had to be cleaned up. Their cat, just like all animals do, knew something alarming was going on, and she was upset. The feeling that someone who was supposed to be there but wasn't hung over the house like an impending storm. Plans had to be canceled, responsibilities not my own had to be taken over, calls had to be made. Did I think my father would die because of a nosebleed? Not really—but it was a weighty possibility. Anyway, I was unsettled. As I have said before, because I was writing this book, I was hyperaware of how—if—I could be cozy in that situation.

Now, look, you won't always be cozy—but one does have to get through. For me, although my bed was made and getting in it would have been an acceptable option—especially after cleaning Dad's blood, lying in bed wasn't going to be cozy for me at that time, even with a cookbook. I immediately changed into my favorite jeans and sweatshirt, even though I'd already been in a similar version of the same outfit. Clothing is not to be underestimated. The weight of a sweatshirt can change the course of your day.

I called my brother again. The first call was just informative, to let him know what was going down—that turned out not to be enough. The second call was to get *real*. "I'm scared. I don't like being left with this. Cleaning blood made me cry," etc., etc. I could say all the stupid things you shouldn't say about grim circumstances that are better handled with stoicism and grace. His deeply familiar voice, even for ten minutes, reminded me of younger days, when Dad wasn't having nosebleeds, gave us both a chance to have a laugh, and made me know that I wasn't in it alone, and neither was he. Coziness can happen in seconds and last for as long, but often results in fortitude.

I cleaned the shit out of the kitchen. I can't control nosebleeds because I'm not an ENT specialist, but I can control my local surroundings, and throwing away moldy cheese from the bottom drawer of the fridge was taking care of *something*.

I cooked barley stew. I had seen the recipe a few days before in the *PS 87 Family Cookbook*, and subconsciously must have twigged that it's a concoction for very cold weather or a disquieting time. Who knew one would arise so suddenly? But there it was. Did I have barley on hand? No, but getting out to the market was an excursion that proved calming because I listened to the radio on the way there, heard Elton John's "Tiny Dancer" (one almost always hears this song on FM radio in the state of Maine), which spoke to my rock-and-roll soul and let it come out. I needed my soul to help my parents, and if Elton John was the one to access it for me, so be it. In trying times, you *need* your best self in order to deal, and sometimes one's best self isn't readily available—sometimes one's worst self rears up. This is natural and okay, but if you can breathe for a minute and call upon the tools of cozy, your wiser self will step forward.

I want to emphasize that the *moments* one takes to find coziness—a familiar song, a look out the window, a doodle on a notepad by the phone—can be moments. Most of us are the captains of the ship and need to lead, take action, mobilize. Coziness is not about lying around. It's the opposite. It's the fuel you need to engage.

THE DRINK

Be sure to heat the earthen pot
And have your water boiling hot
Put in a teaspoon per cup
That each of you intend to sup
Allow to stand for minutes four
Then off the leaves be sure to pour.
When serving put the milk in first,
Add sugar and allay your thirst.
With this delightful, fragrant brew
You'll be refreshed and live anew.
—OLD SCOTTISH RECIPE FOR MAKING TEA

HAVE A MASSIVE mug of tea next to me. Tea, as much as it's about the cup (heavy, delicate, paper, old, handmade), temperature (there really is a moment when hot water cools to a temperature so perfect it feels like a sunrise), flavor, and caffeine, is really an internal nod to my childhood friends. We were forever putting on a kettle—even at age sixteen, and now, decades later, with every cup I drink I feel near to those pals, many of whom don't live close to me. Inside my psyche, some part of adolescence returns to flop on sofas, smoke stupid cigarettes, talk about boys and teachers.

Most everyone I discuss cozy with instantaneously lifts

their pointer finger up in the air and proclaims an undisputable truth about the coziness of the hot drink. My friend Mo said every night growing up, she and her father used to have a cup of hot milk and Ovaltine (a 1970s crumbly, dissolving malt mix) before bed. That memory came out of her mouth so fast it was like she had been waiting her whole life to say it, and then she went on another detailed riff about chai. I think she could have discussed hot liquids for the entire afternoon. It seems for many worldwide, the signet of cozy is a steaming cup.

According to *The Atlantic*, the country where they drink the most tea, measured in pounds per person, is Turkey, with 6.961 pounds per person per year, followed by Morocco, Ireland, Mauritania, the United Kingdom, Seychelles, United Arab Emirates, Kuwait, Qatar, and number ten, Kazakhstan. They have one of those maps that is shaded where tea-drinking populations are the densest. The United States ranks about halfway through that list. The most frequent *coffee* drinkers per capita are found in a completely different set of countries. The top five are Finland, Norway, Iceland, Denmark, and the Netherlands.

Thematically, organization and temperature are at play here. If you ever feel lonely, just think about the millions of people standing in front of a stove waiting for water to boil. The Japanese have elaborate tea ceremonies called *chanoyu* that date back to the sixteenth century; it's an art form, studied and passed down through generations. But even one person in their kitchen in Staten Island or Moscow has drink-related customs. Mugs, whisks, presses, grinds, tea cozies, kettles, even the folded boxes of Twinings teas connect the entire world with inner well-being.

In Morocco, boiling-hot water infused with sweetened, heady mint is poured from way up high into small glasses. The height is needed to create a foam on the top of the dairy-less tea. The drama of the cascading boiling liquid demonstrates how important the simple act of pouring tea is to the culture.

IT'S NOT JUST the libation, it's the vessel. How big or small is your cup? What's the weight of it? Does it fit in the holder in your car? Is it handmade? My favorite tea mug was purchased on a farm in upstate New York. It has a cow illustrated on its side. Peter and I sought refuge at this working farm with our three very small children one fall day many moons ago. When kids are little, farms are *important*—especially for city rats like ours. We were always in search of one. Anyway, after we learned about fertilizer and leaned on fences watching cows, there was a small café with egg sandwiches, the eggs provided by the chickens you had just met. That year, they were also selling mugs. I wish I had bought twenty, because they were never for sale again.

There is nothing like the classic New York City blue-and-white deli coffee cup of my youth. But a few years ago, I started drinking coffee *solely* because of Starbucks holiday cups. I wanted to join the fun-coffee-drink world that appeared to be happening inside those cheery red cups. (Of course, I could've ordered tea and gotten the same cup, but it didn't seem as cool as coffee.) I told a Starbucks barista that story and he said, "Not the first time I've heard it happening to people."

People fall in love over tea, hash ideas, consider their day. My ex-husband and I made a pot of tea to drink while we worked out our financial and custody agreements before we divorced. By the time the pot was done, we had pretty much hammered it out. It was like Earl Grey acted as our mediator. (The only thing my husband Peter knows how to cook is coffee, and he takes it as seriously as doing our taxes. No tea for him, he's not a tea guy.)

When my grandmother died, she was at a hospital in Burlington, Vermont. Apparently, during her last few hours, she recalled her childhood, telling stories about her parents in Boston, the war, France, art, and the many birds she had painted during her life. I wasn't close to my grandmother, for no reason other than in Waspy families sometimes formality and physical distance get in the way. But as I age, I feel close to her, and while I have been writing this book I have thought about her often. Granny didn't have a reputation for being cozy because

she was thought of as difficult, remote, cerebral, introverted, and artistic. She wasn't jolly, effusive, or warm, but that's the thing about coziness—sometimes it's not obvious. In my favorite picture of her she's holding a small bunny, she's smoking, and she has a cup of tea by her side. From her dirty fingers you can see she had been drawing with pastels.

Granny was a little bit psychic, and no-nonsense. She understood and had animals around her always. She had parrots, and many dogs; at one point there was a raccoon and a small owl that lived in the bookshelf. Once we were all sitting on the porch of her red house on the St. Lawrence River, and a bird flew into the window. It was flailing and dying on the wooden floor. She got up from her wicker chair, reached down, took the bird into her birdlike hands, and broke its neck so it wouldn't suffer another second.

I don't think Granny was frightened of death. When she was near the end of her life, my mother was with her and later told me that Granny, during her reflections, softly requested a "small cup of coffee." That has always stayed with me.

MUSIC

"Johnny, rosin up your bow and play your fiddle hard."

—THE CHARLIE DANIELS BAND

Wɪᴛʜ ᴛʜᴇ sᴘᴇᴇᴅ of sound, music, cosmically sublime and profound, is perhaps the fastest way to drill into the truth of who you are. Our son Thomas spends the lion's share of the day playing his guitar. Fortuitously, he was home on the morning I started this chapter—he was figuring out "No Hard Feelings" by the Avett Brothers in his room. I summoned the teenager in. "Well, it's almost too big, but music *is* cozy because you can find emotion in ANY song— even if you don't like it, you can connect to it." First of all, that is sort of the point of the book: finding connection with anything—even if you don't like it. Second, I think it's funny that a teenager would say "finding emotion," when they seem to have so many emotions in them at all times. Anyway, I was going to explode into writing about dancing in rainstorms as the Grateful Dead jammed onstage, or recall memories of my father driving while Stevie Wonder played on the FM radio. Good Lord, just last night I listened to the Dixie Chicks while making tacos for dinner. Can't think of anything more satisfying than that—and yet, Thomas is correct, it kinda feels too big. Music is in the same category in my mind as falling in love or giving birth. But cozy?

Then I remembered this little chunk of rosin I had as a young girl. Mum wanted me to learn the cello, I think because she played. I liked it all right, but I wasn't good at it. Music was hard to read, practicing felt lonely, and I can't even remember my teacher. But I do remember being taken to rent the cello at a musty string instrument store in the West Forties, where the planks of the wooden floor creaked as you followed the owner back, back, back through rows of violas—like Lucy tiptoeing her way through the wardrobe to find Narnia. The same older Eastern European gentleman helped us organize the rental. If you had told me he was Itzhak Perlman's personal violin guy, I would have believed you. After fitting me for the cello and bow, he went behind the glass counter filled with sheet music and pulled out a drawer—it sounded like rocks were being disturbed and rolling around. He pulled out an amber nub and placed it in my hand. It smelled oily and like a pine forest. Mum watched happily (it is fun when your kids are introduced to something that could be life changing) as the man taught me to slide it up and down the fibers on my bow, back and forth, slowly and then quickly. The rosin would make the hair tacky, allowing it to grip the strings of the cello better, ideally so one could produce a clear, pretty sound. I was instructed to do this every time before I played, and I certainly followed directions—rosining the bow was the only reason I practiced.

He gave me a piece of mustard-yellow felt too. I kept the folded felt and rosin in a little velvet box with a lid, which was built into the cello case. I felt so official. If I learned anything during that year of playing cello, it wasn't Bach, it was the ritual of rosining my bow. The tools around the music gave me a pathway in, a little control of something so profound and earthshaking. I feel the same way about the little silver cup Thomas uses to hold his guitar picks. The cup lives in his room, where he plays most. Inside, the medium-hardness picks are at the ready. They lie in wait, ridged and colorful, to be chosen and strummed so he can get lost "finding emotions" in the gigantic, swirling, drowning, life-giving music.

LAST THOUGHT

I WAS THINKING ABOUT religion a lot for this book—it was
keeping me up in the middle of the night. In the knaves,
sahns, and arks; in the lessons and chapters of verse, the
teachings, the oral laws and holy books; the robes and tomes
stored under benches; the rituals, customs, and devotion,
even with the historic and very real modern-day complexities
of religion, coziness can surely be found. Religion appears to
be mostly about connection. Connection to a church, synagogue, or mosque; connection to the leaders; connection
to prayer, God, and yourself. But it's like I couldn't process
it—it was overwhelming.

There are these birch trees I can see outside the window
near the pew where my family sits, in the church I go to in
Maine. Light dapples through the fluttery, summer-green
leaves. Patterns in the white, chalky bark look as if they were
drawn in charcoal by a folk artist, and there must be families of birds perched on all the branches, because their song
sometimes makes it hard to hear the minister. The serenity
I feel imagining those birch trees, even here in New York
City, is probably where I am most familiar with religion. But
is that enough? I'm not qualified.

As I boiled it down and thought, and attempted to hash it out, what became clear was that I wanted to write not about religion, but help. I've received so much of it, and yes, some of the help I've gotten has come from religion of one kind or another, but most of the help I've gotten has come from teachers, therapists, peers, doctors, books, and articles in my local paper, the *New York Times*. If you think about it, help is everywhere, and all of us, at some point, are very much in need of it. A lot of times when you need help, life doesn't feel very cozy.

When darkness falls on your life, whatever kind, the disquiet and heartache can make you feel, as a friend once described it, cosmically alone. I've had moments when I couldn't breathe or open my eyes because of plain old agony. But the thing is, you do end up opening your eyes—in my experience, what comes next, after a bath and a cup of tea, is the business of getting help.

The preamble for Alcoholics Anonymous is,

"Alcoholics Anonymous is a fellowship of men and women who share their experience, strength and hope with each other that they may solve their common problem and help others to recover from alcoholism. The only requirement for membership is a desire to stop drinking. There are no dues or fees for A.A. membership; we are self-supporting through our own contributions. A.A. is not allied with any sect, denomination, politics, organization or institution; does not wish to engage in any controversy, neither endorses nor opposes any causes. Our primary purpose is to stay sober and help other alcoholics to achieve sobriety."

I just looked up meetings in my neighborhood, and on this Sunday alone there were seventeen AA meetings within walking distance spaced evenly through the day. In those walls, there will be a chair to rest, a place to listen, a place to make yourself a cup of coffee, a leader to guide you, and people gathered from all walks of life seeking or providing comfort and support.

As I age, I am certain that seeking assistance from an expert, a friend, or a community is as uncomplicated as turning on the lamp in a dim part of the room. Sure, asking an actual person is bolder, it might require allocating resources, it takes effort and bravery, but as it turns out, humans are perhaps the coziest part of this whole shindig, and they are everywhere. Thinking back, I can't come up with a single time when I asked for help and someone, even a stranger, came up short.

Mostly, the people who didn't come up short were my parents. I wrote a lot of this sitting in their dining room in Maine—in my forties. Every once in a while, Dad would visit me to check out what I was doing. One time, near the end of the summer when the wind had already turned to the northwest, making the air sharper and cooler, I showed him my writing corkboard. It was jammed with three-by-five note cards outlining every cozy idea I could think of, all the themes, all the ways to get to it.

"Why don't you just call this book *Life?*" he said.

I balked. "*Life?* Uh, no. It's called *Cozy*, it's about the truth of who you are and connecting all that to things like movie tickets and dogs and . . . you know?"

He smiled and moved over to the window. Dad looked out at the cobalt-blue sea, the reaching pines, chili-red rose-hips, and the ferry in the distance shuttling people back and forth. "It's gonna be great." I waited for the next sentence when I was sure he would capitulate and say I was correct; all the things I was writing about were just cozy, not as big as life. But he didn't say anything, he just hung out for a while keeping me company.

I think Dad was on to something, as he always has been. Coziness, whatever that is to you, *is* life. It's life at its greatest. It's not always so easy, right? It can be really dark, and

One of these

sad—but there are these moments. When I was a kid, out of nowhere, I would be overcome by a swelling feeling that living on this earth—with animals, rivers, fried shrimp, my transistor radio, my brothers, my roller skates, and the hot New York City pavement—was so fantastic I couldn't believe I got to do it. Most of the time, that sensation was fleeting. But the bursts kept me going, and they still do.

Those moments are everywhere. It's for you to find them.

THE
RECIPES

RECIPES

I SIMPLY CAN'T WRITE a book called *Cozy* and omit a section for recipes. At the close of almost every day, and certainly once during a day, I find refuge in a cookbook. I plan meals I am quite sure I'll never make, glide my hand over the penciled-in notes from years before, sigh with relief looking at the words "chop," "boil," "stir," and "simmer."

In the acknowledgments sections of cookbooks, there is evidence of the collaborative nature of cooking. I am at peace looking at pictures of food, dreaming of flavors to use, and doing the light arithmetic needed to double or triple a recipe.

The recipes here are just ones that floated to the surface as I wrote. I ate a lot of almond butter and strawberry jam sandwiches leaning against the kitchen counter; my family had fried shrimp and zucchini for dinner sometimes as those recipes are so easy and friendly to make while one works. And every time life got hard, it seemed like God or the kitchen sprites left three overripe bananas in the bowl so I could soothe the soul by whipping up a banana bread. A few of the recipes are not mine, but feel like a good fit.

RECILE INDEX

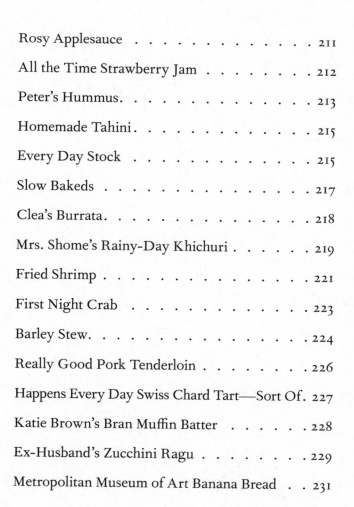

ROSY APPLESAUCE

(LEARNED IT FROM MY MOTHER)

You can feed this pretty applesauce to anyone, from a baby to a grandpa. It's an easy road to feeling like you have taken care of people, starting with the way it makes your kitchen smell as the apples simmer away. The sauce's blush color is part of its charm.

YIELD: 7 or 8 servings, depending on how hungry everyone is

INGREDIENTS

7–8 medium apples, peeled and cored. Choose any kind you like with red skin. (Bite one first to see if you like the flavor!)
Water

Cut the apples into roughly 2-inch chunks. The chunks should be uniform in size so the cooking is even.

Fill a heavy saucepan with 2 inches of water. Tumble apple chunks off the cutting board into water and boil over a medium-low flame. Cover the pot. Check frequently to stir the apples and make sure the water hasn't evaporated. Don't let the apples burn! When the apples have softened so you can mash with the back of your wooden spoon, turn off the flame.

Using an immersion blender, pulverize the apples until the mixture looks like the applesauce of your dreams.

You can eat this warm with vanilla ice cream, cold with potato latkes, or by itself in a dish. Keep in the fridge, covered.

ALL THE TIME STRAWBERRY JAM

This is a case where other people's cozy relationship to something changed who I was. I am one of those raspberry jam people. However, there were so many stories like Laura Ingalls Wilder's Farmer Boy *and movies like* Howards End, *a Merchant Ivory film, where people are forever "slathering" strawberry jam all over toast and scones, that I started to feel jealous of other people's love for it. As a teenager, I watched my friend Catherine put a spoon into a jar of strawberry jam and then right into her mouth. Later, I became obsessed with* The Great British Baking Show, *and, as if they were taunting me, the bakers made strawberry jam from scratch to use as filling in sandwich cakes—push came to shove and one day I bought frozen strawberries at the market and let it rip. One of the coziest cooking experiences in my forty-eight years. Now there will always be a mason jar of it in our fridge, next to the raspberry.*

YIELD: 1 jar

INGREDIENTS

2 15-ounce bags of frozen organic strawberries (of course, if you can get fresh fruit from a farmer's market or garden, that is good too, but when that's not available, I like frozen. It's picked and flash frozen on the fields, which means the nutrition is locked in there!)

1 cup of sugar in the raw

1 lemon

Fill a heavy-bottomed sauce pan with all the berries. Cook for about 5 to 10 minutes until they are mushy and soft.

Add the sugar and squeeze the lemon in. Stir and mix until it begins to bubble and boil. Put the flame to very low and cook for another 20–30 minutes. There is a jam test you can do with a cold plate in the freezer, but I never understood how that works. Just cook it until it looks like jam from the market. Let cool. Sterilize a mason jar in boiling water. Fill up the jar with jam and keep in the fridge for at least three weeks.

PETER'S HUMMUS

I find it cozy to become obsessed with cooking one thing and then ditching it. After I gave birth to my first son, Hugh, I repeatedly baked Anadama bread. After the second, Thomas, was born in May of 2004, I baked granola every week of that summer. I remember it well because Thomas's uncle was a marine and serving in Iraq. With little contact and troubling news from the region of angry fighting and casualties, our family was on edge. The steady habit of baking and then sending the cookie-like cereal overseas was a small comfort, and the only thing I could think to do. Last winter felt like eighteen months, and I must have made three hundred muf-fins. And this year, because my beloved husband really adores it, hummus is a constant in the fridge. Peter would eat it three times a day, and since he can't cook (he does six million other things well in this life), it's good to have a vat of it on hand. I want there to be something I have made at the ready whenever he's hungry. BUT hummus is also a totally cozy food to eat right after it's been whipped up. It's warm, and the dipping is particularly satisfying. For this one I make homemade tahini, which sounds hard, but isn't.

YIELD: This will make a LOT of hummus. Bring the army.

INGREDIENTS

2 15-ounce cans chickpeas
1 clove garlic
1 cup olive oil
1 lemon

1 cup Homemade Tahini
   (page 215)
Salt and pepper

Open cans of chickpeas and drain. Dump into blender. Peel 1 garlic clove and put it in the blender. Add the olive oil. Squeeze the juice of one lemon (or more if you want a lemony hummus) into the mix. BLEND! It should churn and whip into smooth, creamy hummus. Add salt and pepper to taste.

I like to serve this in a bowl, spreading it with a spatula in a circle forming a wide nest. I top the hummus with Kala-mata olives, sliced grape tomatoes, maybe some shaved orange bell pepper, chopped basil, and snipped chives over it all. Anything you have in the fridge that's fresh and bright is a good contrast to the earthy bean mix. At the very end, drizzle with more olive oil. Have a box of great crackers or toasted pita bread to scoop it all up with. Cozy to stand at the counter with a glass of wine while whipping this up for supper.

HOMEMADE TAHINI

1 cup sesame seeds
Salt and pepper to taste

3 tablespoons grapeseed oil

Heat a heavy frying pan over a low flame and pour hulled white sesame seeds into it. Shake and jiggle around until you start to smell them. It's a nutty aroma. Watch out! It's very easy to burn sesame seeds (and all nuts) because of their high oil content. Don't let them brown. They should be a light tan color at most. Pour them in a blender. Add a teaspoon of salt and hearty grinds of pepper. Turn the blender on and slowly pour in grapeseed oil (I have also used olive oil; it's just a bit of a heavier flavor) until it starts to look smooth and blended. You may have to stick the end of a wooden spoon in there to help it along.

EVERY DAY STOCK

This is the stock from the butternut squash soup in the beginning of the book. Once you start having good stock around, you will make a million dishes you never thought you would make. I think stock may even be called "bone broth," which is quite trendy now, and people who sip it say it's restorative and very cozy. I use stock for soups, curries, and pasta sauces. You can buy ingredients intentionally to make stock, but I tend to make use of what I have left over in the fridge.

YIELD: 8 cups

INGREDIENTS

All the bones from a roasted chicken (but really, you can use any kind of bones you have around, AND if you are a vegetarian, you can use Parmesan rinds instead of bones)

1–2 leeks or onions with skins on (I love leeks, they are a star in our kitchen—I freeze the dark ends of the leaves specifically for making stock. But onions are also a good choice—the skins create a deep golden color when boiled)

1 stalk celery

1 big carrot

2–3 sprigs rosemary

2–3 sprigs thyme

1–2 bay leaves

A small handful peppercorns

Dump any combination of the above items into a large pot, fill it with water, and set it on the stove until it comes to a full boil. Reduce to a simmer, cover the pot, and let it sit there gently bubbling for three to six hours. The longer you simmer, the more flavor will develop. You can tell it's done when there is a rich color and it's reduced a few inches. Let the pot cool on the stove, strain into a glass container, and either put in the fridge to use in the next day or two or freeze for the future.

SLOW BAKEDS

* * *

(LEARNED IT FROM MY MOTHER)

For as long as I can remember, slow-baked tomatoes have been a staple in our family's meal rotation. What's brilliant about them, besides being absolutely delicious, is that you can cook this dish in the dead of winter with the hardest, most terrible tomatoes that you would never put in a salad or eat by themselves. As is true with the applesauce and stock, the smell of these cooking away in the oven will make you feel like you are Julia Child. So cozy to have something in the oven for the better part of an afternoon.

YIELD: Serves 4

INGREDIENTS

4 tomatoes (don't have to be gorgeous)	1 tablespoon olive oil
	Salt and pepper

Preheat oven to 250 degrees. Wash and take the vine top out of each tomato. Slice in half on the fat side. Arrange the halves in rows on a rimmed baking sheet. Coat the tomatoes with olive oil. Generously season with salt and pepper. Slide into oven and bake for at least 2 hours until they are bubbling, wilted, and glistening. You can cook them for 3 hours if you want more intense flavor.

Serve with eggs, fish, chicken, beef—almost anything. Hard to mess up, and they keep in fridge beautifully for leftovers.

CLEA'S BURRATA

◢ ◢ ◢

I met Clea Lewis in the schoolyard on our kids' first day of kindergarten. Perhaps making a friend like Clea is one reason I find schoolyards cozy. In any case, she thinks carefully about what she is serving and to whom. One fall day yonks ago, Clea; her husband, Peter; and their boys came over for dinner and to play touch football. Out of her market bag, Clea pulled a container with one egg-like ball of cheese resting in cold water. Chatting away, she gently poured the cheese into her hand over the sink, letting the cold water fall through her fingers, and rolled it onto a big plate. Then she tumbled olives and sliced radishes on the cheese, glugged good olive oil over the whole thing, opened a box of fantastic crackers, and said, "Okay, let that sit for a while and then we can all scoop." And scoop we did. This is community food.

YIELD: serves 4–6

INGREDIENTS

8 ounces fresh, fresh, fresh burrata cheese (check the expiration date and give a good smell before serving)

20 sliced grape tomatoes

a handful of olives

4 radishes, thinly sliced

1–2 shaved orange or red bell peppers

a handful fresh herbs such as basil, mint, or chives

4–6 tablespoons very good olive oil

salt and pepper to taste

Burrata is buffalo milk cheese. It's baseball-sized and serves about four people to have with drinks or as part of a summery lunch (truth be told, we eat this in every season). There's a layer of firm mozzarella on the outside, and inside is creamy, softer, rich cheese, which is why it is a fabulous scooping food. You buy it in cold water, but it's served at room temperature. I chop tomatoes ahead of time, drizzle olive oil and grind salt on them, and let that mixture get delicious. I like shaving peppers with a mandolin. I am sort of going crazy lately shaving vegetables over almost everything we eat, but the method really works with this dish because you want everything you throw on top of this cheese to be close to melting in your mouth.

At the end I snip chives, basil, or mint (or all three) over the mountain of goodness. Let it sit and then serve with your most favorite cracker. I have been eating crackers made of seeds lately; a friend with Celiac disease turned us on to them. I'm not gluten free, but these things are a crunchy delight and really great for scooping.

MRS. SHOME'S RAINY-DAY KHICHURI

In the last two years of thinking about and writing this book, I've asked a ton of people what is cozy to them. My friend Mo and I go to IKEA together about twice a year. For New Yorkers, driving to New Jersey feels like a bit of a Thelma & Louise road trip. I roll up in the minivan to pick her up in the morning. Mo is always standing there with tea and two packages of something good to eat (one time she brought me a kouign-amann, a glorious pastry that will blow your mind—well worth waiting on line for them). We wind our way up the avenues of the Upper West Side and drive across the George Washington Bridge, chatting mostly about our kids, jobs, and husbands. On one trip, I asked her what she found cozy and she said, "My mom's khichuri. Every day that it rained, when I was walking home from school, I knew for sure we would have khichuri. I didn't appreciate it then but make it now for my kids on rainy days. And I love it with extra dal and less rice. And with mango pickle on the side."

You can zuhz it up if you like, but this is the basic recipe.

YIELD: serves 4

INGREDIENTS

1 cup mung dal	1 teaspoon grated ginger
2 tablespoons oil	1 teaspoon raw sugar
3 cloves	1 teaspoon salt
3 green cardamom pods	½ cup cut beans
2 bay leaves	½ cup cauliflower florets
1 piece cinnamon	½ cup frozen peas
2 green chilies	½ cup cubed potatoes
1 cup basmati rice	2 tablespoons ghee
1 teaspoon turmeric	

In large pan, dry roast dal for 3 minutes; wash and set aside. In same pan, add 2 tablespoons oil.

Add whole spices, and when it splutters, add washed rice and fry for 2 minutes. Add dal and fry for 1 minute. Add turmeric, ginger, sugar, and salt and stir for 2 minutes. Add 5 cups of water and bring to boil, cover, and cook for 2 minutes. Add all vegetables, cover, and cook for 15 minutes, adding a little more water if needed. Turn off heat and add the ghee or a pat of butter on top.

Khichuri done. Serve with papad or omelet or pakora and mango pickle.

FRIED SHRIMP

We play this game where you have to choose what three meals you would eat every day for the rest of your life. Mine are huevos rancheros for breakfast with a scone and jam on the side, a BLT and green puree soup for lunch, and fried shrimp for dinner. I was introduced to scampi when I was fourteen on a trip to Wales with my parents and brother Andrew. Scampi (or fried shrimp) was on every pub menu, and I ordered it every time. It came with mashed potatoes and peas. I feel like the luckiest girl in the world whenever I make or eat it.

(Note: I try my best to find shrimp that have the least negative impact on the environment. Sometimes that means the shrimp come frozen, but there are some markets that think about a healthy ocean and sell either fished or farmed seafood. I think it's worth it to ask the fishmonger or look on the packaging.)

YIELD: serves 4

INGREDIENTS

16 ounces big (but not huge) shrimp

6 glugs grapeseed oil

¼ cup flour

Salt and pepper to taste

Once you have defrosted or cleaned your shrimp, dry them. I use a gigantic cast-iron skillet for this because you want the shrimp to have room to react to the heat, but use any heavy skillet you have. You might have to do this in batches—but it's fast because they are shrimp. Slosh those 6 glugs of oil in the bottom of the pan so it's heavily coated, with about a quarter inch of oil at the bottom.

Dump the flour into a brown paper bag and add plenty of salt and pepper. Drop in the towel-dried shrimp and give it a shake. Place the flour-coated shrimp in the hot, oily pan. You want to hear and see a sizzle.

Cook for 2–3 minutes until the bottoms are beautifully brown. Turn over and cook for about a minute more. They should look inviting, crispy, and have good color. Heat is your friend here—get that oil hot! But be careful. Season again while the shrimp are hot.

I serve this with something like a tomato salad, slow-baked tomatoes, a green salad, sometimes polenta, or I pile the shrimp on a toasted baguette and load that up with some cole slaw, or sometimes I'll serve this with creamed spinach or black beans . . . Goodness, how I love fried shrimp.

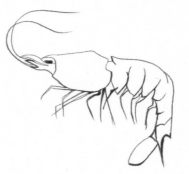

FIRST NIGHT CRAB

Having a go-to is cozy. Something you know works, you know people adore, and you could do with your eyes closed. Dependability—it's the same reason why uniforms are cozy. I'm putting in this recipe as MY go-to, but if you don't have access to fresh crab, or you are allergic, etc., I ask you to think about what your go-to is. What's your slam dunk? Maybe you can write it in the margins of this page if somehow crab isn't your thing.

My parents live on an island in Maine. So right-out-of-the-sea crab is our go-to for a special occasion. Whenever someone arrives at the house for the first time in the summer, we serve First Night Crab.

YIELD: Serves 4–6

INGREDIENTS

Rice

2 16-ounce packages
   frozen peas

Olive oil, salt, and pepper
   to taste

2 8-ounce cups fresh
   crabmeat

16 fluid ounces heavy
   whipping cream

Make white rice. This is not an easy task for me—if there is ANYONE else around, including my dogs, I might ask them to make it. Uncle Ben's is fine, but so is some lovely jasmine or basmati variety. At the same time, gently steam the frozen peas. Once they are just warmed and still a pretty green, drizzle a little olive oil over the peas and season with salt and pepper.

ke your crabmeat (which should only smell like the sea; n't use if there is any fishy smell at all) and drain it of any water. Tumble it in a heavy-bottomed saucepan, and pour in cream until it almost covers the crab. Over a medium/ low flame, stir gently until the mixture is very hot, but not boiling. Season lightly with salt and black pepper.

On each plate, serve a mound of rice and ladle the crab and cream over it. A spoonful of peas goes right on the side. Serve with ground pepper and salt on the table. And maybe a crusty baguette to sop up whatever is left on the plate.

BARLEY STEW

There are a number of reasons I am including this recipe. One, Scotland. Two, I ate a lot of this as a child and so I believe any child will eat a lot of it—mine did. And three, because I submitted it for the PS 87 Family Cookbook a few years back (tested and edited by star New York City chef Bill Telepan, who was a parent—my pride about that sweet project hasn't diminished). If there is anything cozier than an institutional cookbook where anyone can contribute, I know not.

YIELD: serves 4 with leftovers

INGREDIENTS

8 cups organic stock (you can use one you made from this book—page 215)

2 cups water

1 cup pearl barley

2 leeks (white and light-green sections very thinly sliced)

Salt and pepper

2 stalks celery, chopped

2 carrots chopped into
½-inch rounds

2 medium potatoes or
turnips cut into
½-inch cubes

2 cups cooked stew meat—
beef, pork loin,
shredded roast, chicken,
turkey, or chickpeas for
a vegetarian option

Chopped parsley

In a large pot, combine stock, water, pearl barley, and sliced leeks over medium-high heat and bring to a boil. Stir and reduce heat to low so that the stew maintains a gentle simmer for about 45 minutes. Season to taste with salt and pepper and stir now and again.

When barley is tender, add the celery, carrots, and potatoes or turnips. Cook for another 20–30 minutes. Everything should be tender—this is nursery food. Add the cooked meat and heat through. If it all gets too thick, add more stock or water. Just before serving, stir in chopped parsley.

Serve in bowls with hot, good bread, or toasted rye with butter or a hunk of Brie cheese. If you have wooden spoons to eat it with, that would be fun.

REALLY GOOD PORK TENDERLOIN

✦ ✦ ✦

Leftovers are cozy, and after all is said and done with this for lunch or dinner, this pork is a leftover situation, especially for sandwiches. For that reason, I always make more than is necessary.

YIELD: serves 4–6 with leftovers

INGREDIENTS

1 8-ounce jar of good Dijon mustard

3 heaping tablespoons curry powder (you can use more or less as you like. I want to taste the curry, but not be overpowered by it)

½ cup olive oil (or more if needed)

4 or 5 of the best pork tenderloins you can get (farmers are hip to how easy tenderloin is to make at home, and they often have them at the farmer's market. For the sake of our dear earth, try to find pigs that have been humanely raised)

Salt and pepper to taste

Dump entire jar of mustard in a bowl. Add curry powder. Glug the olive oil in and mix around until you have something in between a paste and sour cream consistency.

Rinse tenderloins and pat dry. Place them on the cookie sheet in a row, not touching. My cookie sheet is big enough to fit 5 with a good 2 inches between. Then heavily coat (I use my hands) the pork with your mustard-curry mixture, covering every inch. Drizzle a little more olive oil and season with salt and pepper. Turn on the broiler.

During this next part, you are dancing with the heat. I slide the cookie tray into the middle of the oven. The broiler will cook the meat from the top. You want to let it get beautifully brown and roasted, and then you take the tray out and rotate the meat so another side cooks. You do this until all sides of the loins are really crispy and brown, charred a bit. I like my pork cooked through, so if you are unsure if it's done (I can feel by pressing the meat with my finger), the internal temperature should read 145 degrees. Take out of oven and let rest for a good 10 minutes.

Slice in 1½-inch pieces and serve.

I serve this with Major Grey's chutney and my version of raita (full-fat Greek yogurt, grated cucumbers, lemon, and dill), salad, polenta, cole slaw, lentils . . . Anything tastes good with this.

HAPPENS EVERY DAY
SWISS CHARD TART—SORT OF

There is a part in my first book where I describe making this savory tart. It's from French Vegetarian Cooking *by Paola Gavin. People have often asked me for the recipe, and so here it is—sort of! I'm having trouble finding the author to ask permission, so unfortunately I can't give you the EXACT recipe. This will count as an imaginative and experimental recipe. Goes something like this: Buy a savory pie crust, par-bake it for ten minutes; during this time, sauté onions, add sliced tomatoes, and make a mookie (seasoning with salt and pepper all the while); set that mixture aside on a plate and sauté Swiss chard in same pan. Thinly slice Gruyère cheese. Assemble in par-baked pie crust, layer starting with greens on bottom and ending with the cheese on top. Bake in 375 degree oven for 45 minutes. Best made in the early fall when tomatoes and chard are being harvested.*

I have this with salad with snipped chives and a glass of red wine or cold apple cider.

KATIE BROWN'S BRAN MUFFIN BATTER

As promised in the home chapter, here is Katie Brown's amazing muffin batter mix. When I first ate these fluffy beauties, they were right out of the oven. And that's the whole point to me—the batter is waiting in the fridge for you! Katie's mother, Mrs. Brown, swears that this batter will keep for two months in a tightly sealed container, but Katie can only attest to two weeks. She doesn't really know though because in her house the demand for these is so great that once made, the batter gets baked up almost immediately. The thought of having batter in the fridge on hand is, well, out of hand.

INGREDIENTS

1½ cups sugar

½ cup Crisco (yes, I am from the Midwest and we use Crisco)

2 eggs

2 cups buttermilk

2½ cups flour

2½ teaspoons soda

1 teaspoon salt

3 cups Kellogg's All-Bran

1 teaspoon salt

1½ cups raisins (I rarely put these in and my mom uses white raisins)

Cream the sugar and the Crisco together, then cream two eggs. Add the buttermilk alternately with the dry ingredients till it is all mixed together. Bake at 350 degrees for 25 minutes either all together in a batch or a few at a time, leaving the rest of the batter in a tightly sealed glass container.

EX-HUSBAND'S ZUCCHINI RAGU

One thing that is cozy is when you get along with ex-spouses. It may take months or years, but eventually, if you can work it out, well, that's good. This is my ex-husband's recipe, and it is the favorite and most requested dish I make for my step-daughter, Sage. Something about that turn of events feels a bit cosmic to me.

YIELD: serves 4

INGREDIENTS

8–10 zucchini (smaller zucchini are better for this; mediums are good too. Zucchini have a lot of water in them—a lot. So they need to drain and they will cook down)

Salt

2 cloves garlic

4 glugs olive oil

Fresh ground pepper

A hunk of Parmesan cheese

Before you get started, make sure you have a handheld mandolin. You can slice with a knife too, of course, and I did for years, but mandolins when used carefully are wildly effective in the kitchen.

Using the mandolin, thinly slice zucchini into a large colander. After you finish slicing each zucchini, sprinkle or grind a layer of salt over it. Do this until all the zucchini are sliced and the colander is full. Let sit in sink for 30 minutes. Lots of the water will drain out of the vegetables.

Smash garlic cloves with the side of a big knife and slice. Heat olive oil in a large heavy-bottomed pan over medium-high flame. Put the garlic in and jiggle around until you can smell the nuttiness coming out. Do not let brown! Add all the zucchini. Toss and stir this around, cooking it down and down and down. Add ground pepper. You can maintain a high-ish flame for this as the zucchini likes what the heat does. Almost at the end, the ragu of squash should look melty and like a mush. Grind good Parmesan over it, mix in, and grate on some more.

I eat this on toast, over spaghetti, as a side with anything, or cold the next day standing in front of the fridge. You can squeeze lemon on it if you like or have it with chopped fresh herbs like chives or basil.

METROPOLITAN MUSEUM OF ART
BANANA BREAD

In the 1970s, my mother worked in the drawings department of the Metropolitan Museum of Art. While there, she helped compile and edit a book called A Culinary Collection: Recipes from the Members of the Board of Trustees and Staff of The Metropolitan Museum of Art. *Throughout my childhood, we ate food from this gem of a book, and now, like it's my job, I make Amy Blumenthal's banana bread at least once a week. It seems when things are blue or tough, there are always three rotting bananas in the kitchen. It's cozy to get through a hard spot by baking, and what I bake is this.*

YIELD: 1 loaf

INGREDIENTS

3 overripe bananas

1 cup sugar

1 egg

1½ cups flour

4 tablespoons butter

1 teaspoon baking soda

1 teaspoon salt

Preheat oven to 325 degrees. Peel bananas and mash with a fork and stir in the rest of the ingredients. Pour into buttered Teflon pan. Bake for 1 hour.

Warm out of the oven is one thing; toasted with butter the next day is next level. Don't forget the tea.

ACKNOWLEDGMENTS

AS I STARTED thinking about this book, my treasured friend and agent, Bill Clegg, and I walked arm in arm in the Highline in New York City, and together we listed everything we could think of that was cozy. Food things, like donuts, sad things like broken hearts, and of course we exclaimed very loudly, at the same time, that walking arm in arm is cozy! There is never a day that goes by that I don't thank heaven and earth for the wonderful Bill Clegg.

When I first met with Karen Rinaldi to talk about this book, we drank tea on a sofa. During that meeting not only did Karen totally get what I was talking about, but while deftly honing my ideas, also gave parenting advice, spoke like a poet about surfing and the ocean (she has a seahorse tattoo), and made the true point that this book would be a big collaboration—kind of with the world. I would like to thank Karen for giving *Cozy* a shot, her spectacular points of view, her kindness, and her sense of fun.

In the same first meeting, but on a different sofa, sat Sarah Murphy and Hannah Robinson, and for that I am so grateful. Sarah Murphy with careful wisdom and a good pencil brought much-needed structure to *Cozy*. Hannah Robinson, with boundless positivity and the best possible questions, carried *Cozy* over the finish line. My sincerest thanks to you both.

I would like to give heartfelt thanks to everyone at HarperWave for their hard work, creativity, and support. Copy editor Janet Rosenberg, Joanne O'Neill for designing the cover of leaves and shine!, Penny Makras, the marketing director, and Rachel Elinsky, the publicity director.

Just as Karen predicted, it took just about my whole world to get this book on its feet, and indeed, I am forever grateful to all who contributed their ideas, thoughts, and mojo.

I would like to wholeheartedly and with great love thank Vanessa Gillespie, Bess Ratliff, Mark and Charlotte Cunningham, Nina Train, Ann Riley Finck, RN, Rachel Martin, Dr. Africa Stewart, David Beer FAIA, Clea Lewis, Sarah Durham and her artsy family, Dr. Fred Ogden, Dewi and Robert de Luxembourg, Tracy Zwick, Katie Brown, Miles Redd, Mo Shome, Camilla Calimandrei, Nathan Turner, Eric Hughes, Marina Connor, Annette Berkery, Lindsey Marx, Ali Wentworth, Mariska Hargitay and Peter Hermann, Ashley McDermott, Christine Marinoni, Nick Paumgarten, Cristina Cuomo, Debra Messing, Nancy Jarecki, Sam Sifton, Carmen Duntan, DeSales Harrison, Ann Harrison. Thank you to every old and new friend I have. I am so grateful for you.

Thank you, dearest, always supportive family-in-law, every single one, especially Ellen and Stanley Lattman.

To my parents, brothers and sisters-in-law, nieces and nephews, thank you, loving family. I'm positive this whole cozy thing started in Big Bluesy.

Duke and Maude, always by my side.

Thank you, Hugh, Sage, and Moosey for everything you contributed to this book. Nothing would be cozy without you three spectacular individuals. Stay coze, my knunkers.

Peter, thank you, dear husband, for your love and support. I couldn't have written this book, or any book, without you—that is true. I also can't get our road trip last summer out of my head. Remember when we sang "True Sadness" by the Avett Brothers driving on that great highway in Idaho? We were looking out at the road ahead and sang in unison— loudly. That was cozy. I am so grateful to be in unison with you and looking in the same direction.

I asked friends, "What's cozy to you?"

Grocery shopping, hooks to hang things on, Dr. Seuss books, snow days, old paperbacks, cats, having a meeting place, garlic cut up in olive oil, shells, museum cafeterias, the smell of my street in the morning, bath dragons, prayer, emojis, sleeping on trains, cold martinis, composting, painting in a studio, fudge, putting on an apron, everything in order, butchers, jigsaw puzzles, oatmeal raisin cookies, sound of a dishwasher running after dinner, smell of my grandfather's house, water, having a friend live across the street, hammocks, getting makeup done, anything French, family dinner, my pickup truck, thinking about my parents in synagogue, post-surf sit on the beach, leftovers for breakfast, sound of kids talking in the other room, calling someone a genius, an oven mitt, the paths in Central Park, first sip of coffee, the shade, à La Colombe black & tan with a bodega bacon, egg, and cheese, succulent gardens, the smell of elementary school classrooms, circular tables, eating an egg standing up, ponds, babies on their stomachs, pizza in bed, carrying something small with you, photo albums, crayons, the billowing trail of a jet plane, when things are shaped to fit a corner, *New York Times* Cooking website, Christmas carols, minivans, carving wax, tying sneakers, clogs, dogs drinking water, cashmere socks, Boulevardiers, Smartwool socks, pulling on an ear, looking up movie times, baking pie, waiting in the wings of a theater, front pocket of my backpack, packing what I want, newspapers delivered to my door, getting into a warm bed, falling in love, birding, favorite jeans, reading to Ije, maple syrup, heated maple syrup, any bookstore anywhere, beans and rice, rice and dal, sewing name tags, a well-walked dog, ryokans, beeswax, candles, sitting by the fire (quite a few people said this), reading glasses, my hat.

What do *you* think is cozy?

ABOUT THE AUTHOR

ISABEL GILLIES is the *New York Times* bestselling author of *Happens Every Day, A Year and Six Seconds,* and *Starry Night.* Her work has been published in *Vogue,* the *New York Times, Real Simple, Cosmopolitan,* goop, and *Saveur.* A lifelong New Yorker and actress for many years, she lives in Manhattan with her husband, three kids, and two dogs.